Interactive Notebooks
LANGUAGE ARTS

Grade 8

Credits

Author: Sara Haynes Blackwood
Content Editors: Elise Craver, Chris Schwab, and Angela Triplett

Visit *carsondellosa.com* for correlations to Common Core, state, national, and Canadian provincial standards.

Carson-Dellosa Publishing, LLC
PO Box 35665
Greensboro, NC 27425 USA
carsondellosa.com

978-1-4838-3131-2
01-341157784

Table of Contents

What Are Interactive Notebooks?

Interactive notebooks are a unique form of note taking. Teachers guide students through creating pages of notes on new topics. Instead of being in the traditional linear, handwritten format, notes are colorful and spread across the pages. Notes also often include drawings, diagrams, and 3-D elements to make the material understandable and relevant. Students are encouraged to complete their notebook pages in ways that make sense to them. With this personalization, no two pages are exactly the same.

Because of their creative nature, interactive notebooks allow students to be active participants in their own learning. Teachers can easily differentiate pages to address the levels and needs of each learner. The notebooks are arranged sequentially, and students can create tables of contents as they create pages, making it simple for students to use their notebooks for reference throughout the year. The interactive, easily personalized format makes interactive notebooks ideal for engaging students in learning new concepts.

Using interactive notebooks can take as much or as little time as you like. Students will initially take longer to create pages but will get faster as they become familiar with the process of creating pages. You may choose to only create a notebook page as a class at the beginning of each unit, or you may choose to create a new page for each topic within a unit. You can decide what works best for your students and schedule.

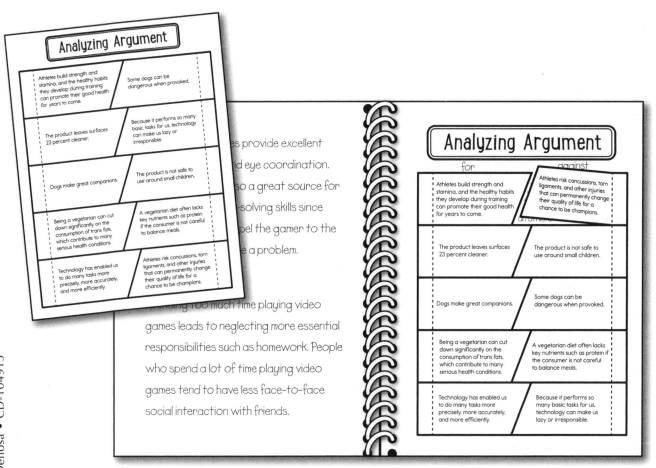

A student's interactive notebook for analyzing argument

Getting Started

You can start using interactive notebooks at any point in the school year. Use the following guidelines to help you get started in your classroom. (For more specific details, management ideas, and tips, see page 10.)

1. Plan each notebook.

Use the planning template (page 9) to lay out a general plan for the topics you plan to cover in each notebook for the year.

2. Choose a notebook type.

Interactive notebooks are usually either single-subject, spiral-bound notebooks, composition books, or three-ring binders with loose-leaf paper. Each type presents pros and cons. See page 5 for a more in-depth look at each type of notebook.

3. Allow students to personalize their notebooks.

Have students decorate their notebook covers, as well as add their names and subjects. This provides a sense of ownership and emphasizes the personalized nature of the notebooks.

4. Number the pages and create the table of contents.

Have students number the bottom outside corner of each page, front and back. When completing a new page, adding a table of contents entry will be easy. Have students title the first page of each notebook "Table of Contents." Have them leave several blank pages at the front of each notebook for the table of contents. Refer to your general plan for an idea of about how many entries students will be creating.

5. Start creating pages.

Always begin a new page by adding an entry to the table of contents. Create the first notebook pages along with students to model proper format and expectations.

This book contains individual topics for you to introduce. Use the pages in the order that best fits your curriculum. You may also choose to alter the content presented to better match your school's curriculum. The provided lesson plans often do not instruct students to add color. Students should make their own choices about personalizing the content in ways that make sense to them. Encourage students to highlight and color the pages as they desire while creating them.

After introducing topics, you may choose to add more practice pages. Use the reproducibles (pages 78–96) to easily create new notebook pages for practice or to introduce topics not addressed in this book.

Use the grading rubric (page 11) to grade students' interactive notebooks at various points throughout the year. Provide students copies of the rubric to glue into their notebooks and refer to as they create pages.

What Type of Notebook Should I Use?

Spiral Notebook

The pages in this book are formatted for a standard one-subject notebook.

Pros

- Notebook can be folded in half.
- Page size is larger.
- It is inexpensive.
- It often comes with pockets for storing materials.

Cons

- Pages can easily fall out.
- Spirals can snag or become misshapen.
- Page count and size vary widely.
- It is not as durable as a binder.

Tips

- Encase the spiral in duct tape to make it more durable.
- Keep the notebooks in a central place to prevent them from getting damaged in desks.

Composition Notebook

Pros

- Pages don't easily fall out.
- Page size and page count are standard.
- It is inexpensive.

Cons

- Notebook cannot be folded in half.
- Page size is smaller.
- It is not as durable as a binder.

Tips

- Copy pages meant for standard-sized notebooks at 85 or 90 percent. Test to see which works better for your notebook.

Binder with Loose-Leaf Paper

Pros

- Pages can be easily added, moved, or removed.
- Pages can be removed individually for grading.
- You can add full-page printed handouts.
- It has durable covers.

Cons

- Pages can easily fall out.
- Pages aren't durable.
- It is more expensive than a notebook.
- Students can easily misplace or lose pages.
- Larger size makes it more difficult to store.

Tips

- Provide hole reinforcers for damaged pages.

How to Organize an Interactive Notebook

You may organize an interactive notebook in many different ways. You may choose to organize it by unit and work sequentially through the book. Or, you may choose to create different sections that you will revisit and add to throughout the year. Choose the format that works best for your students and subject.

An interactive notebook includes different types of pages in addition to the pages students create. Non-content pages you may want to add include the following:

Title Page

This page is useful for quickly identifying notebooks. It is especially helpful in classrooms that use multiple interactive notebooks for different subjects. Have students write the subject (such as "Language Arts") on the title page of each interactive notebook. They should also include their full names. You may choose to have them include other information such as the teacher's name, classroom number, or class period.

Table of Contents

The table of contents is an integral part of the interactive notebook. It makes referencing previously created pages quick and easy for students. Make sure that students leave several pages at the beginning of each notebook for a table of contents.

Expectations and Grading Rubric

It is helpful for each student to have a copy of the expectations for creating interactive notebook pages. You may choose to include a list of expectations for parents and students to sign, as well as a grading rubric (page 11).

Unit Title Pages

Consider using a single page at the beginning of each section to separate it. Title the page with the unit name. Add a tab (page 78) to the edge of the page to make it easy to flip to the unit. Add a table of contents for only the pages in that unit.

Glossary

Reserve a six-page section at the back of the notebook where students can create a glossary. Draw a line to split in half the front and back of each page, creating 24 sections. Combine Q and R and Y and Z to fit the entire alphabet. Have students add an entry as each new vocabulary word is introduced.

Formatting Student Notebook Pages

The other major consideration for planning an interactive notebook is how to treat the left and right sides of a notebook spread. Interactive journals are usually viewed with the notebook open flat. This creates a left side and a right side. You have several options for how to treat the two sides of the spread.

Traditionally, the right side is used for the teacher-directed part of the lesson, and the left side is used for students to interact with the lesson content. The lessons in this book use this format. However, you may prefer to switch the order for your class so that the teacher-directed learning is on the left and the student input is on the right.

It can also be important to include standards, learning objectives, or essential questions in interactive notebooks. You may choose to write these on the top-left side of each page before completing the teacher-directed page on the right side. You may also choose to have students include the "Introduction" part of each lesson in that same top-left section. This is the *in, through, out* method. Students enter *in* the lesson on the top left of the page, go *through* the lesson on the right page, and exit *out* of the lesson on the bottom left with a reflection activity.

The following chart details different types of items and activities that you could include on each side.

Left Side Student Output	Right Side Teacher-Directed Learning
• learning objectives • essential questions • I Can statements • brainstorming • making connections • summarizing • making conclusions • practice problems • opinions • questions • mnemonics • drawings and diagrams	• vocabulary and definitions • mini-lessons • folding activities • steps in a process • example problems • notes • diagrams • graphic organizers • hints and tips • big ideas

Planning for the Year

Making a general plan for interactive notebooks will help with planning, grading, and testing throughout the year. You do not need to plan every single page, but knowing what topics you will cover and in what order can be helpful in many ways.

Use the Interactive Notebook Plan (page 9) to plan your units and topics and where they should be placed in the notebooks. Remember to include enough pages at the beginning for the non-content pages, such as the title page, table of contents, and grading rubric. You may also want to leave a page at the beginning of each unit to place a mini table of contents for just that section.

In addition, when planning new pages, it can be helpful to sketch the pieces you will need to create. Use the following notebook template and notes to plan new pages.

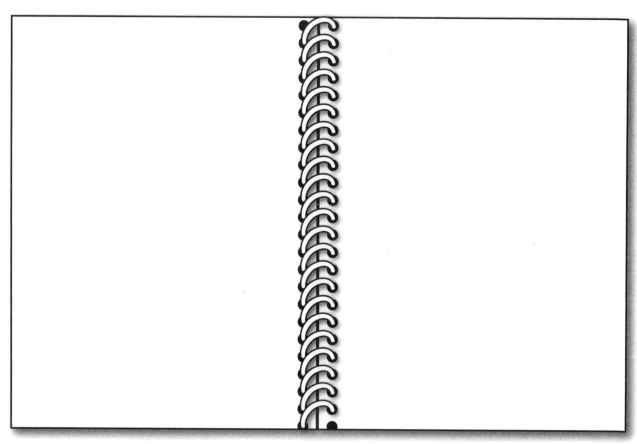

Left Side   **Right Side**

Notes

_____

_____

_____

Interactive Notebook Plan

Page	Topic	Page	Topic
1		51	
2		52	
3		53	
4		54	
5		55	
6		56	
7		57	
8		58	
9		59	
10		60	
11		61	
12		62	
13		63	
14		64	
15		65	
16		66	
17		67	
18		68	
19		69	
20		70	
21		71	
22		72	
23		73	
24		74	
25		75	
26		76	
27		77	
28		78	
29		79	
30		80	
31		81	
32		82	
33		83	
34		84	
35		85	
36		86	
37		87	
38		88	
39		89	
40		90	
41		91	
42		92	
43		93	
44		94	
45		95	
46		96	
47		97	
48		98	
49		99	
50		100	

Managing Interactive Notebooks in the Classroom

Working with Younger Students

- Use your yearly plan to preprogram a table of contents that you can copy and give to students to glue into their notebooks, instead of writing individual entries.

- Have assistants or parent volunteers precut pieces.

- Create glue sponges to make gluing easier. Place large sponges in plastic containers with white glue. The sponges will absorb the glue. Students can wipe the backs of pieces across the sponges to apply the glue with less mess.

Creating Notebook Pages

- For storing loose pieces, add a pocket to the inside back cover. Use the envelope pattern (page 81), an envelope, a jumbo library pocket, or a resealable plastic bag. Or, tape the bottom and side edges of the two last pages of the notebook together to create a large pocket.

- When writing under flaps, have students trace the outline of each flap so that they can visualize the writing boundary.

- Where the dashed line will be hidden on the inside of the fold, have students first fold the piece in the opposite direction so that they can see the dashed line. Then, students should fold the piece back the other way along the same fold line to create the fold in the correct direction.

- To avoid losing pieces, have students keep all of their scraps on their desks until they have finished each page.

- To contain paper scraps and avoid multiple trips to the trash can, provide small groups with small buckets or tubs.

- For students who run out of room, keep full and half sheets available. Students can glue these to the bottom of the pages and fold them up when not in use.

Dealing with Absences

- Create a model notebook for absent students to reference when they return to school.

- Have students cut a second set of pieces as they work on their own pages.

Using the Notebook

- To organize sections of the notebook, provide each student with a sheet of tabs (page 78).

- To easily find the next blank page, either cut off the top-right corner of each page as it is used or attach a long piece of yarn or ribbon to the back cover to be used as a bookmark.

© Carson-Dellosa • CD-104915

Interactive Notebook Grading Rubric

4
- _____ Table of contents is complete.
- _____ All notebook pages are included.
- _____ All notebook pages are complete.
- _____ Notebook pages are neat and organized.
- _____ Information is correct.
- _____ Pages show personalization, evidence of learning, and original ideas.

3
- _____ Table of contents is mostly complete.
- _____ One notebook page is missing.
- _____ Notebook pages are mostly complete.
- _____ Notebook pages are mostly neat and organized.
- _____ Information is mostly correct.
- _____ Pages show some personalization, evidence of learning, and original ideas.

2
- _____ Table of contents is missing a few entries.
- _____ A few notebook pages are missing.
- _____ A few notebook pages are incomplete.
- _____ Notebook pages are somewhat messy and unorganized.
- _____ Information has several errors.
- _____ Pages show little personalization, evidence of learning, or original ideas.

1
- _____ Table of contents is incomplete.
- _____ Many notebook pages are missing.
- _____ Many notebook pages are incomplete.
- _____ Notebook pages are too messy and unorganized to use.
- _____ Information is incorrect.
- _____ Pages show no personalization, evidence of learning, or original ideas.

Inference

Introduction

Show students a variety of pictures and ask questions that are not directly answered by the content of the photos. Have students cite specific details that validate their answers. For example, ask them what season it must be in a picture of people cooking out in shorts. Then, have them attempt to answer questions in the same way when there is no way they could know the answers. For example, ask students to explain the relationship between two people in a picture who are walking together. Have students explain (verbally or in writing) the difference between the first set of guesses and the second. Use their explanations to define inference on the board.

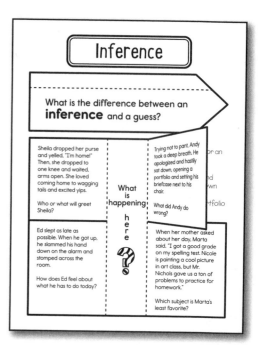

Creating the Notebook Page

Guide students through the following steps to complete the right-hand page in their notebooks.

1. Add a Table of Contents entry for the Inference pages.

2. Cut out the title and glue it to the top of the page.

3. Cut out the definition flap. Apply glue to the back of the top section and attach it below the title.

4. Under the definition flap, explain the difference between an inference and a guess. (Answers will vary but may include that an inference uses information from the text to make a logical conclusion.)

5. Cut out the flap book. Cut on the solid lines to create four flaps. Apply glue to the back of the center section and attach it below the definition flap.

6. Write the answer to the question and two key words or phrases from the text that support your answer under each flap.

Reflect on Learning

To complete the left-hand page, have students recount situations where they made inferences in real life. Have students write the story as a narrative first. Then, have them write the clues they used to make the inference. Finally, have them write the inference.

Inference

What is the difference between an **inference** and a guess?

Sheila dropped her purse and yelled, "I'm home!" Then, she dropped to one knee and waited, arms open. She loved coming home to wagging tails and excited yips.

Who or what will greet Sheila?

Trying not to pant, Andy took a deep breath. He apologized and hastily sat down, opening a portfolio and setting his briefcase next to his chair.

What did Andy do wrong?

What is happening here

Ed slept as late as possible. When he got up, he slammed his hand down on the alarm and stomped across the room.

How does Ed feel about what he has to do today?

When her mother asked about her day, Marta said, "I got a good grade on my spelling test. Nicole is painting a cool picture in art class, but Mr. Nichols gave us a ton of problems to practice for homework."

Which subject is Marta's least favorite?

Incorrect Inferences

Have students listen as you describe a situation they might see outside a window and ask them to guess what is happening. Make sure each situation could have multiple right answers. For example, if the window is wet, someone may have just washed it, a sprinkler may have sprayed it, or it could have rained. Have students write or discuss how much evidence they might need to feel confident that an inference is correct.

Creating the Notebook Page

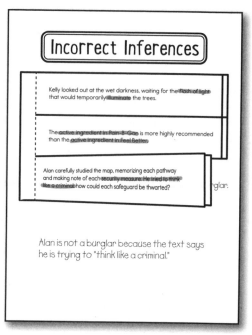

Guide students through the following steps to complete the right-hand page in their notebooks.

1. Add a Table of Contents entry for the Incorrect Inferences pages.

2. Cut out the title and glue it to the top of the page.

3. Cut out the two flap books. Cut on the solid lines to create three flaps on each book. Apply glue to the gray glue section of the larger flap book and place the smaller flap book on top to create a stacked six-flap book. Apply glue to the back of the left section of the flap book and attach it to the page.

4. Read each top flap. Then, read the flap below it to see an incorrect inference that an inattentive reader might make. Under the second flap, write a more accurate inference than the one given on the second flap.

5. Highlight or underline the word(s) on the top flap that reinforce the new inference and prove the original inference wrong.

6. At the bottom of the page, choose one set of words that you highlighted and write a sentence to explain the inference.

Reflect on Learning

To complete the left-hand page, have students explain how it would affect a reader's understanding to continue the story under the impression that the original inference was correct.

Incorrect Inferences

Kelly looked out at the wet darkness, waiting for the flash of light that would temporarily illuminate the trees.

The active ingredient in Pain-B-Gon is more highly recommended than the active ingredient in Feel Better.

Alan carefully studied the map, memorizing each pathway and making note of each security measure. He tried to think like a criminal: how could each safeguard be thwarted?

It is nighttime; Kelly is waiting for someone to turn on a flashlight.

Pain-B-Gon is more highly recommended than other medications with the same active ingredient.

Alan is a burglar trying to figure out how to steal a heavily guarded item.

glue

Summarizing

Introduction

Have students write a paragraph about a scenario they have all experienced, such as the first day of school, lunch, or a fun time with a friend. Point out that students were not able to recount every detail or word from the whole event, forcing them to choose only the most important parts to retell. Explain that this decision-making process is called *summarizing*.

Creating the Notebook Page

Guide students through the following steps to complete the right-hand page in their notebooks.

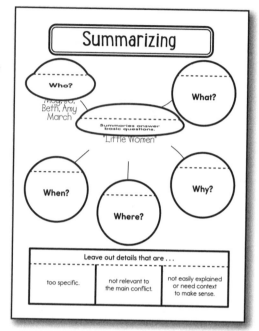

1. Add a Table of Contents entry for the Summarizing pages.

2. Cut out the title and glue it to the top of the page.

3. Cut out the *Summaries* flap. Apply glue to the back of the top edge and attach it in the center of the page.

4. Under the flap, write the title of a text you have recently read.

5. Cut out the *who, what, when, where,* and *why* flaps. Apply glue to the back of the top section of each circle and attach them around the *Summaries* flap. Draw a line from each of the *who, what, when, where,* and *why* flaps to the *Summaries* flap to create a bubble chart.

6. Under the flaps in the bubble chart, write the relevant details of the text, naming characters under the *who* flap, the setting under the *where* and *when* flaps, the major conflict under the *what* flap, and what motivates the characters or creates the conflict under the *why* flap.

7. Cut out the flap book. Cut on the solid lines to create three flaps. Apply glue to the back of the top section and attach it to the bottom of the page.

8. Under the flaps in the flap book, record the requested details.

Reflect on Learning

To complete the left-hand page, have students write a short summary of the book they used to complete the right-hand page. Students should use the details from the bubble chart flaps without including any details from the flap book to write their summaries.

Summarizing

Who?

What?

When?

Where?

Why?

Leave out details that are . . .

too specific.	not relevant to the main conflict.	not easily explained or need context to make sense.

Summaries answer basic questions.

Paraphrasing

Introduction

Define *paraphrasing* as rephrasing the original thought or text into one's own words. Discuss the three R's of paraphrasing: **R**eword (replace words and phrases with synonyms when possible), **R**earrange (rearrange words within sentences to make new sentences), and **R**echeck (the paraphrase should convey the same meaning as the original text). Then, place students into pairs and ask a question such as, "What did you do before coming to school this morning?" or "Tell where you would like to go on vacation and why you would like to go there." One partner should answer the question in three or four sentences. The other partner should paraphrase the student's answer. Then, have the partners switch roles.

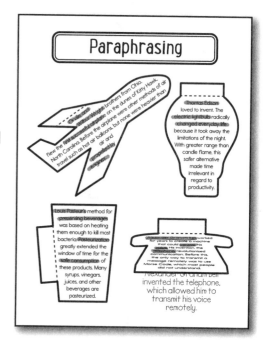

Creating the Notebook Page

Guide students through the following steps to complete the right-hand page in their notebooks.

1. Add a Table of Contents entry for the Paraphrasing pages.

2. Cut out the title and glue it to the top of the page.

3. Cut out the flaps. Apply glue to the back of the tab on each flap and attach the flaps to the page in any order, making sure they do not overlap.

4. Read each flap. Then, highlight or underline key words or phrases from the passage.

5. Under each flap, write a sentence that paraphrases the same information and includes the key words from the flap.

Reflect on Learning

To complete the left-hand page, have students list situations where paraphrasing is more effective than recounting a story or conversation word for word. For each situation on their lists, have them explain why paraphrasing would be a more efficient or preferable option.

Paraphrasing

Thomas Edison loved to invent. The electric lightbulb radically changed everyday life because it took away the limitations of the night. With greater range than candle flame, this safer alternative made time irrelevant in regard to productivity.

Orville and Wilbur Wright, brothers from Ohio, flew the first successful airplane on the dunes of Kitty Hawk, North Carolina. Before the airplane were other methods of air travel such as hot air balloons, but none were heavier than air and propelled by engines.

Louis Pasteur's method for preserving beverages was based on heating them enough to kill most bacteria. Pasteurization greatly extended the window of time for the safe consumption of these products. Many syrups, vinegars, juices, and other beverages are pasteurized.

Alexander Graham Bell worked for years to create a machine that could transmit his voice. His invention, the telephone, revolutionized communication. Before this, the only way to transmit a message remotely was to use Morse Code, which most people did not understand.

Textual Evidence

Introduction

Choose four sentences from a paragraph and number them 1, 2, 3, and 4. Post a sheet of paper in each corner of the room so that each corner corresponds with one of the sentences. Have students read the paragraph. Then, ask them factual questions that they can answer with one of the four sentences. Rather than answer aloud, students should go to the corner that corresponds with the number of the correct sentence. Have a student who went to the correct corner confirm the answer for the class. Point out to students that they are using the author's words (textual evidence) to show the answer instead of their own words.

Creating the Notebook Page

Guide students through the following steps to complete the right-hand page in their notebooks.

1. Add a Table of Contents entry for the Textual Evidence pages.

2. Cut out the title and glue it to the top of the page.

3. Cut out the three pockets. Apply glue to the back of the tabs on each pocket and attach the pockets to the bottom third of the page.

4. Cut out the sentence strips.

5. Read each sentence and sort them into groups that make sense. For each group of strips, develop a statement that is directly supported by all of the sentences. Write the statement on one pocket and place the appropriate strips in the pocket. Repeat this step with the other pockets. No strips should be left over.

Reflect on Learning

To complete the left-hand page, have students write a statement about photography that is not supported by the sentence strips from the right-hand page. Have students write an explanation of why the statement is not supported by the textual evidence.

Answer Key
Answers will vary, but potential statements include "photos can serve many purposes," "photography can be a profession," and "cameras have changed over time." (A potential thesis statement might be, "Photography equipment has changed over time, but the demand for personal and professional photographs remains.")

Textual Evidence

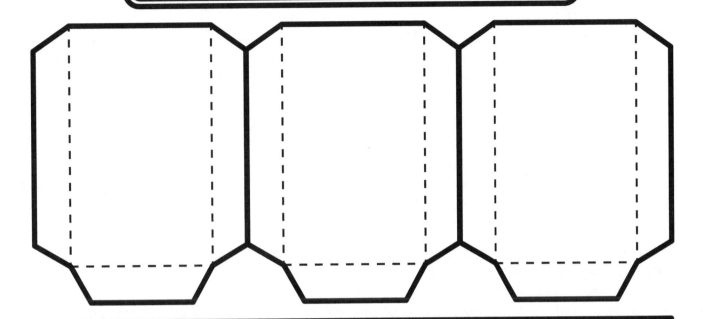

Many people enjoy taking photographs that show unique perspectives.

Some people take photographs for a living.

Photographers get paid for taking professional pictures at weddings, concerts, and other events.

Photographers can also be paid for photos documenting historic or newsworthy events.

Photos used to be recorded on film and then developed from the film pieces called negatives.

Digital pictures preserve images as files on memory cards.

Cameras can be simple, one-time-use devices or complex, expensive pieces of equipment.

The quality of a digital picture is determined by how many megapixels the camera has.

Photos can preserve once-in-a-lifetime events or just fun moments.

Many people like to take or display pictures of their loved ones.

Structure

Introduction

In groups, have students create towers from several predetermined classroom objects that vary greatly in weight (textbook, notebook paper, ruler, etc.). Have students compare and contrast their towers. Although the details of their towers will vary, students will likely find that most of them built their towers with the heaviest items at the bottom. Explain that the building process for writing is very similar and writers can use structure to organize information, create excitement, or build suspense in a text. Explain that just like the way towers are built is called *structure*, authors build a text by *structure* as well.

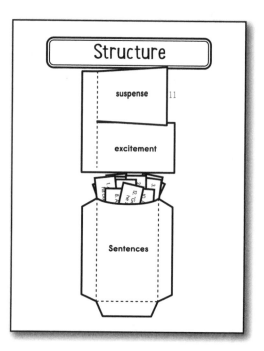

Creating the Notebook Page

Guide students through the following steps to complete the right-hand page in their notebooks.

1. Add a Table of Contents entry for the Structure pages.

2. Cut out the title and glue it to the top of the page.

3. Cut out the flap book. Cut on the solid line to create two flaps. Apply glue to the back of the left section and attach it to the page below the title.

4. Cut out the pocket. Apply glue to the back of the tabs and attach it to the page below the flap book.

5. Cut out the sentence strips.

6. Arrange the sentences to create a story with suspense. Use the numbers to write the sentence order you used under the *suspense* flap. You may use or disregard any sentences you deem appropriate.

7. Repeat step 6 to create a story that reflects excitement. Write the sentence order you used under the *excitement* flap. When finished, place the sentence strips in the pocket.

Reflect on Learning

To complete the left-hand page, have students choose one of the stories they created with the sentence strips from the right-hand page. Students should write to add details to complete the story. Allow time for students to share their work.

Structure

1. Antoine couldn't sit still through any of his classes.	2. His birthday has always been his favorite day of the year.
3. He burst into the apartment, looking around wildly.	4. His father laughed and said, "Don't forget, you'll have a surprise waiting here for you after school!"
5. He danced through his shower and sang to his cereal spoon.	6. "Mom! Dad! Where are you?" Antoine shouted.
7. Antoine peered into the living room, not sure what he would see.	8. Antoine woke up and jumped out of bed.
9. "We're in the living room," his parents replied.	10. At lunch, his friends gave him high fives.
11. There stood his whole family, smiling! They all shouted, "Happy birthday, Antoine!"	12. "Good morning, Mom!" he trumpeted as he zoomed into the living room.

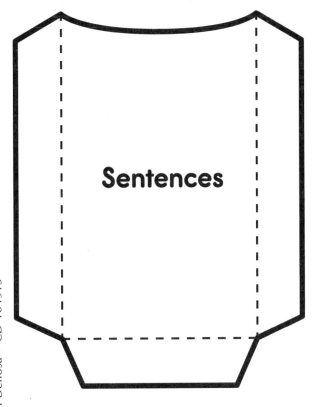

Sentences

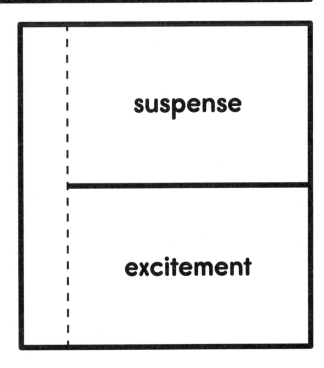

suspense

excitement

Connotation

Introduction

Have students create lists: one for *good* words and one for *bad* words. Circle words from their lists that can actually be good or bad, or words that are only positive or negative in connotation, not denotations. Use a dictionary to help students compare the actual definitions (denotations) of the circled words to the connotations (the feelings associated with the words that prompted students to label each word as *good* or *bad*).

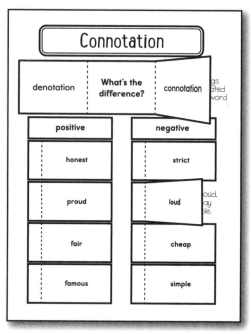

Creating the Notebook Page

Guide students through the following steps to complete the right-hand page in their notebooks.

1. Add a Table of Contents entry for the Connotation pages.

2. Cut out the title and glue it to the top of the page.

3. Cut out the *What's the difference?* flap book. Apply glue to the back of the center section and attach it below the title.

4. Write the definition for each term under the appropriate flap. (Connotation has to do with feelings associated with a word. Denotation is the strict dictionary meaning of a word.)

5. Cut out the *positive* and *negative* labels and glue them below the flap book to create two columns.

6. Cut out each word flap. Decide whether the connotation of the word is positive or negative, apply glue to the back of the left section, and attach it in the appropriate column.

7. Under each flap, use a detail from the denotation of the word to explain why it has a positive or negative connotation associated with it.

Reflect on Learning

To complete the left-hand page, have students write a paragraph to explain why one of the words from the introduction or the right-hand page has a connotation that differs from its denotation. For example, many people might feel that *strict* is negative because they feel that someone who holds them to a high standard may also be cruel or mean.

Connotation

denotation	What's the difference?	connotation

positive	negative
strict	honest
cheap	loud
fair	proud
famous	simple

Supporting Textual Evidence

Read students a short story and have them pinpoint the details that helped them understand what a character is like (characterization) and what will cause the character to act (conflict). Have students explain how they came to know those details about the character—did the author tell them, or did they figure it out based on what the character did or said? Have students decide how the qualities revealed by the author affected the character's response to the conflict. Have students use the details they identified when characterizing the protagonist to explain their answers.

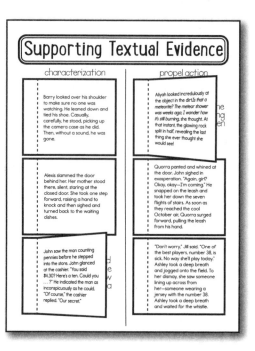

Creating the Notebook Page

Guide students through the following steps to complete the right-hand page in their notebooks.

1. Add a Table of Contents entry for the Supporting Textual Evidence pages.

2. Cut out the title and glue it to the top of the page.

3. Draw a T-chart on the page. Label one side *characterization* (details that reflect a character's personality and qualities) and the other side *propel action* (details that move the plot forward by causing characters to act or changing the circumstances of the story).

4. Cut out the six flaps. Apply glue to the back of the left sections and attach them below the appropriate headings.

5. Under each flap in the *characterization* column, explain how you know that the purpose of that piece of evidence is to show what a character is like. Under each flap in the *propel action* column, explain how you know that the purpose of that piece of evidence is to move the plot forward.

Reflect on Learning

To complete the left-hand page, write a short paragraph that describes a situation in a way that reveals what the main character is like. Write a second short paragraph that describes the same scene but focuses on the action of the situation.

Supporting Textual Evidence

Barry looked over his shoulder to make sure no one was watching. He leaned down and tied his shoe. Casually, carefully, he stood, picking up the camera case as he did. Then, without a sound, he was gone.

Alexis slammed the door behind her. Her mother stood there, silent, staring at the closed door. She took one step forward, raising a hand to knock and then sighed and turned back to the waiting dishes.

"Don't worry," Jill said. "One of the best players, number 38, is sick. No way she'll play today." Ashley took a deep breath and jogged onto the field. To her dismay, she saw someone lining up across from her—someone wearing a jersey with the number 38. Ashley took a deep breath and waited for the whistle.

John saw the man counting pennies before he stepped into the store. John glanced at the cashier. "You said $4.30? Here's a ten. Could you . . . ?" He indicated the man as inconspicuously as he could. "Of course," the cashier replied. "Our secret."

Aliyah looked incredulously at the object in the dirt. *Is that a meteorite? The meteor shower was weeks ago; I wonder how it's still burning*, she thought. At that instant, the glowing rock split in half, revealing the last thing she ever thought she would see!

Quorra panted and whined at the door. John sighed in exasperation. "Again, girl? Okay, okay—I'm coming." He snapped on the leash and took her down the seven flights of stairs. As soon as they reached the cool October air, Quorra surged forward, pulling the leash from his hand.

Literary Devices

Introduction

Define a literary device as *a specific language an author uses to have an intended effect on his audience.* Review each of the literary devices on the right-hand page. Then, divide the class into six groups. Assign one of the six literary devices to each group. Decide on a predetermined amount of time and instruct each group to look for and write as many examples of their assigned literary devices that they can find in classroom materials in the alloted time. Allow time for each group to share one of their examples and explain what kind of effect the literary device has on them as readers.

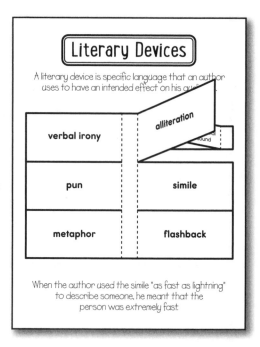

Creating the Notebook Page

Guide students through the following steps to complete the right-hand page in their notebooks.

1. Add a Table of Contents entry for the Literary Devices pages.

2. Cut out the title and glue it to the top of the page.

3. Write the definition for a literary device below the title. (Answers will vary but may include that a literary device is specific language an author uses to have an intended effect on his audience.)

4. Cut out the flap book. Cut on the solid lines to create six flaps. Apply glue to the back of the center section and attach it to the center of the page.

5. Cut out the six flaps. Apply glue to the back of the right or left section of each flap and attach it under the flap of the literary device it defines.

6. Cut out the example pieces. Glue them to the page under the corresponding definition flaps.

7. At the bottom of the page, choose one figurative language example and explain the difference between what the author said and what the author meant.

Reflect on Learning

To complete the left-hand page, have students try to describe a person or place using only literary devices. Then, have students write a physical description of the same person or place that is completely devoid of literary devices. Each student should write a sentence to describe how the inclusion of the figurative language impacts the description.

verbal irony	alliteration
pun	simile
metaphor	flashback

when a speaker says the opposite of what is meant	She is as fast as lightning.
a play on words	He is a cheetah on the track.
comparison by stating one thing *is* another	She remembered the first time she had heard that song.
repetition of an initial consonant sound	A boiled egg is a hard snack to beat.
comparison using "like" or "as"	Peter Piper picked a peck of pickled peppers.
a reflection on the past that interrupts the current action	Please continue to make fun of my hard work.

Literary Devices

Dramatic Irony

Introduction

Have one volunteer step outside of the room momentarily. Then, make a small but reasonably noticeable change in the classroom. Allow the student to return and ask five *yes* or *no* questions to help her guess what change was made. Repeat the process with a new volunteer. Have both volunteers describe the difference between being part of the *act* and part of the *audience*. Then, define dramatic irony as *when the audience knows more about a situation than some or all of the characters do.*

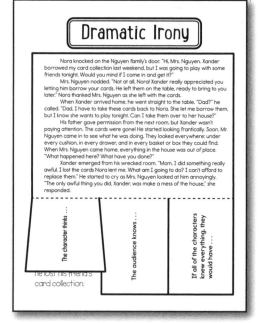

Creating the Notebook Page

Guide students through the following steps to complete the right-hand page in their notebooks.

1. Add a Table of Contents entry for the Dramatic Irony pages.

2. Cut out the title and glue it to the top of the page.

3. Cut out the flap book. Cut on the solid lines to create three flaps. Apply glue to the back of the story section and attach it vertically to the page.

4. Read the story. Under each flap, use details from the story to describe the element of the story listed on the flap.

Reflect on Learning

To complete the left-hand page, have students write a short story where dramatic irony affected a major event or decision for the character or characters. Allow time for students to share their work.

Dramatic Irony

Nora knocked on the Nguyen family's door. "Hi, Mrs. Nguyen. Xander borrowed my card collection last weekend, but I was going to play with some friends tonight. Would you mind if I come in and get it?"

Mrs. Nguyen nodded. "Not at all, Nora! Xander really appreciated you letting him borrow your cards. He left them on the table, ready to bring to you later." Nora thanked Mrs. Nguyen as she left with the cards.

When Xander arrived home, he went straight to the table. "Dad?" he called. "Dad, I have to take these cards back to Nora. She let me borrow them, but I know she wants to play tonight. Can I take them over to her house?"

His father gave permission from the next room, but Xander wasn't paying attention. The cards were gone! He started looking frantically. Soon, Mr. Nguyen came in to see what he was doing. They looked everywhere: under every cushion, in every drawer, and in every basket or box they could find. When Mrs. Nguyen came home, everything in the house was out of place. "What happened here? What have you done?"

Xander emerged from his wrecked room. "Mom, I did something really awful. I lost the cards Nora lent me. What am I going to do? I can't afford to replace them." He started to cry as Mrs. Nguyen looked at him annoyingly. "The only awful thing you did, Xander, was make a mess of the house," she responded.

The character thinks . . . .

The audience knows . . . .

If all of the characters knew everything, they would have . . . .

Plot Choices

Introduction

Have students write a short story that is clearly set on a beach in the year 2030, at a fair in the 1950s, or in a school in the 1970s. Have them do so without using any of the information in the prompt you gave them. For example, they should not use the word *beach, fair, school,* or name the year. Instead, they should use circumstances to make these details evident. Have students highlight the words or details they included to show the details from the prompt. Then, have students underline a moment where a character made a decision or was forced to act. Finally, have them circle a word, phrase, or sentence that describes their characters (physical description or personality traits). Have students discuss the choices they made as authors to get their points across. Point out that an author has to craft certain situations carefully to preserve her main message. Sometimes, authors add details or conflicts, called plot devices, that only exist to serve these purposes.

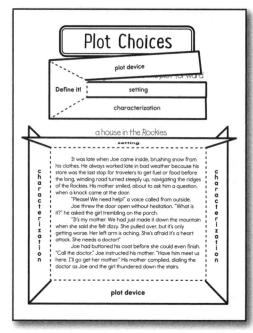

Creating the Notebook Page

Guide students through the following steps to complete the right-hand page in their notebooks.

1. Add a Table of Contents entry for the Plot Choic es pages.

2. Cut out the title and glue it to the top of the page.

3. Cut out the small flap book. Cut on the solid lines to create three flaps. Apply glue to the back of the *Define it!* section and attach it below the title.

4. Write the definitions for plot device, setting, and characterization under the flaps.

5. Cut out the large flap book. Cut on the solid lines to create four flaps. Apply glue to the back of the center section and attach it to the page.

6. Read the story. Under the flaps, write the details from the passage that show the setting, a plot device used by the author, and at least two character traits for Joe.

Reflect on Learning

To complete the left-hand page, have students predict what will happen next in the story based on the text. They should use details from the text to justify their responses.

© Carson-Dellosa • CD-104915

Plot Choices

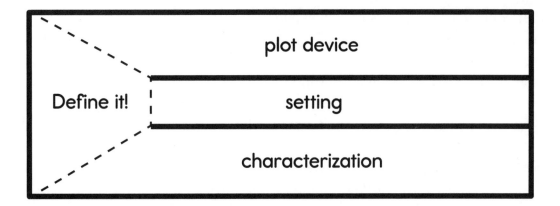

Define it!

plot device
setting
characterization

---

setting

c h a r a c t e r i z a t i o n

It was late when Joe came inside, brushing snow from his clothes. He always worked late in bad weather because his store was the last stop for travelers to get fuel or food before the long, winding road turned steeply up, navigating the ridges of the Rockies. His mother smiled, about to ask him a question, when a knock came at the door.

"Please! We need help!" a voice called from outside.

Joe threw the door open without hesitation. "What is it?" he asked the girl trembling on the porch.

"It's my mother. We had just made it down the mountain when she said she felt dizzy. She pulled over, but it's only getting worse. Her left arm is aching. She's afraid it's a heart attack. She needs a doctor!"

Joe had buttoned his coat before she could even finish. "Call the doctor," Joe instructed his mother. "Have him meet us here. I'll go get her mother." His mother complied, dialing the doctor as Joe and the girl thundered down the stairs.

c h a r a c t e r i z a t i o n

plot device

Theme

Introduction

Read a fable to the class. After the reading, discuss how the fable ends with the moral of the story which is its theme. Read another fable without revealing the moral of the story. Have students guess what the theme could be citing textual evidence to support their answers. Explain that a theme is a lesson or concept that a majority of readers could apply in their own lives. It should not be just one word such as *love*. The theme should not be something the reader could not apply in his own life. Finally, define the purpose of a theme as *to give the reader a sense of the central idea of the piece.*

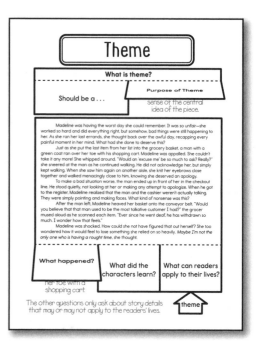

Creating the Notebook Page

Guide students through the following steps to complete the right-hand page in their notebooks.

1. Add a Table of Contents entry for the Theme pages.

2. Cut out the title and glue it to the top of the page.

3. Cut out the *What is theme?* flap book. Cut on the solid line to create two flaps. Apply glue to the back of the top section and attach it below the title.

4. Complete the sentence under the first flap of the *What is theme?* flap book (lesson or idea that can apply to most readers). Under the second flap, write the purpose of theme (to give the reader a sense of the central idea of the piece).

5. Cut out the story flap book. Cut on the solid lines to create three flaps. Apply glue to the back of the story section and attach it to the page.

6. Read the story. Answer the questions about the story under the flaps.

7. Cut out the theme arrow and glue it so that it points to the question that best demonstrates the theme of the story. Note that even though the questions are all similar, only one answer will be able to be labeled *theme*.

8. Write a sentence at the bottom of the page to explain why only that question can yield theme (as opposed to the other two).

Reflect on Learning

To complete the left-hand page, have students write to explain the theme of their favorite movie, providing evidence from the movie. They should use the three questions from the flap book to determine if they have the correct answer.

Theme

theme

What is theme?	
Should be a . . .	Purpose of Theme

Madeline was having the worst day she could remember. It was so unfair—she worked so hard and did everything right, but somehow, bad things were still happening to her. As she ran her last errands, she thought back over the awful day, recapping every painful moment in her mind. What had she done to deserve this?

Just as she put the last item from her list into the grocery basket, a man with a green coat ran over her toe with his shopping cart. Madeline was appalled. She couldn't take it any more! She whipped around. "Would an 'excuse me' be so much to ask? Really?" she sneered at the man as he continued walking. He did not acknowledge her, but simply kept walking. When she saw him again on another aisle, she knit her eyebrows close together and walked menacingly close to him, knowing she deserved an apology.

To make a bad situation worse, the man ended up in front of her in the checkout line. He stood quietly, not looking at her or making any attempt to apologize. When he got to the register, Madeline realized that the man and the cashier weren't actually talking. They were simply pointing and making faces. What kind of nonsense was this?

After the man left, Madeline heaved her basket onto the conveyor belt. "Would you believe that that man used to be the most talkative customer I had?" the grocer mused aloud as he scanned each item. "Ever since he went deaf, he has withdrawn so much. I wonder how that feels."

Madeline was shocked. How could she not have figured that out herself? She too wondered how it would feel to lose something she relied on so heavily. *Maybe I'm not the only one who is having a rough time,* she thought.

What happened?	What did the characters learn?	What can readers apply to their lives?

More about Theme

Introduction

Have students write a story that teaches their classmates the importance of a particular school rule without ever actually sharing the rule. Have other students guess what rule the story is meant to teach, using details from the story to support their answers. Point out that the school rule is serving as the theme of the story and that the details students use to support their answers are plot details that the author included for the purpose of communicating that theme.

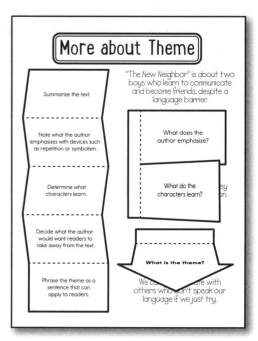

Creating the Notebook Page

Guide students through the following steps to complete the right-hand page in their notebooks.

1. Add a Table of Contents entry for the More about Theme pages.

2. Cut out the title and glue it to the top of the page.

3. Cut out the accordion piece. Fold on the dashed lines, alternating the fold direction. Apply glue to the back of the last section and attach it to the left side of the notebook page.

4. Below the title, write a short summary of a text chosen by your teacher.

5. Cut out the flap book. Cut on the solid line to create two flaps. Apply glue to the back of the left section and attach it below the summary.

6. Cut out the arrow flap. Apply glue to the back of the top section and attach it to the bottom of the page.

7. Answer the questions about the text chosen by your teacher under the flaps. Use the steps from the accordion fold and the answers you wrote under the flaps to help you determine the theme. Write it under the flap.

Reflect on Learning

To complete the left-hand page, have students reflect on why authors might use a story to convey a theme instead of just writing the theme itself.

More about Theme

Summarize the text.

Note what the author emphasizes with devices such as repetition or symbolism.

Determine what characters learn.

Decide what the author would want readers to take away from the text.

Phrase the theme as a sentence that can apply to readers.

What does the author emphasize?

What do the characters learn?

What is the theme?

Central Idea

Introduction

Have students plan a party with a particular motif. (Avoid using the word *theme* as it may confuse students to use the word *theme* in this context.) Ask them whether they will include certain items, making sure to include both items that do and do not work with the motif. Point out to students that in the same way, when they attempt to support the central idea in their writing, they must eliminate irrelevant or contradictory items.

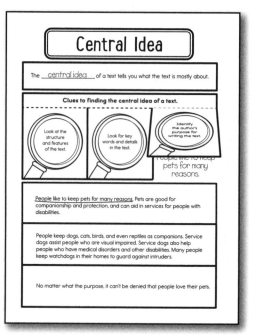

Creating the Notebook Page

Guide students through the following steps to complete the right-hand page in their notebooks.

1. Add a Table of Contents entry for the Central Idea pages.

2. Cut out the title and glue it to the top of the page.

3. Cut out the definition piece and glue it below the title. Read and complete the explanation. (The **central idea** of a text tells you what the text is mostly about.)

4. Cut out the *Clues to finding* flap book. Cut on the solid lines to create three flaps. Apply glue to the back of the top section and attach it to the page.

5. For each flap, use the clue to find the central idea of a text you have read recently. Record your findings under the correct flap.

6. Cut out the three text pieces. Read the text and then decide which piece contains the central idea and underline it. Arrange the text in the correct order and glue the pieces to the page.

Reflect on Learning

To complete the left-hand page, have students choose one of the supporting sentences from the text pieces and write a new paragraph that uses that sentence as its central idea.

Central Idea

The _____ of a text tells you what the text is mostly about.

Clues to finding the central idea of a text.

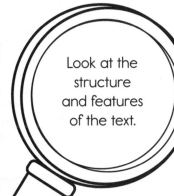

Look at the structure and features of the text.

Look for key words and details in the text.

Identify the author's purpose for writing the text.

People like to keep pets for many reasons. Pets are good for companionship and protection, and can aid in services for people with disabilities.

No matter what the purpose, it can't be denied that people love their pets.

People keep dogs, cats, birds, and even reptiles as companions. Service dogs assist people who are visually impaired. Service dogs also help people who have medical disorders and other disabilities. Many people keep watchdogs in their homes to guard against intruders.

Analyzing Central Idea

Have students draw a scene that includes a person, an animal, an item, and a building or natural element. Have other students guess which of the items in the picture is supposed to be the focus of the "story" the picture tells, using details from the drawing to support their answers. Size, color, position, and other elements of the drawing could all be factors. Analyze with students how the central idea is developed by the details in the drawing. Have students discuss how the details they cite show how the elements of the "story" work together and interact with each other.

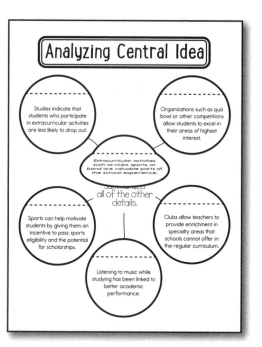

Creating the Notebook Page

Guide students through the following steps to complete the right-hand page in their notebooks.

1. Add a Table of Contents entry for the Analyzing Central Idea pages.

2. Cut out the title and glue it to the top of the page.

3. Cut out the flaps. Decide which one is the central idea ("Extracurricular activities such as clubs, sports, or band are valuable parts of the school experience."). Apply glue to the back of the top section and attach it to the center of the page. Position the other flaps in a circle around the central idea by applying glue to the back of each top section and attaching them to the page. Draw a line to connect each detail to the central idea.

4. Under the central idea flap, write why that sentence is the central idea. Under each of the other flaps, explain how that sentence supports the central idea.

Reflect on Learning

To complete the left-hand page, have students write two more sentences that would support the central idea from the web. Have students explain how their new sentences support the central idea.

Analyzing Central Idea

Listening to music while studying has been linked to better academic performance.

Studies indicate that students who participate in extracurricular activities are less likely to drop out.

Extracurricular activities such as clubs, sports, or band are valuable parts of the school experience.

Clubs allow teachers to provide enrichment in specialty areas that schools cannot offer in the regular curriculum.

Organizations such as quiz bowl or other competitions allow students to excel in their areas of highest interest.

Sports can help motivate students by giving them an incentive to pass: sports eligibility and the potential for scholarships.

Crafting Arguments

Introduction

Have students write a short paragraph about the best movie ever made and give several supporting details. Then, have students highlight or underline the sentences that show what criteria they used to make their determinations. Poll the class to see how many students used concrete factors (such as box office sales, awards won, or ratings from reviewers or critics) and how many used abstract opinions or standards (such as stating that action movies are better than romantic comedies).

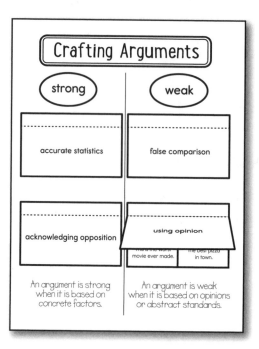

Creating the Notebook Page

Guide students through the following steps to complete the right-hand page in their notebooks.

1. Add a Table of Contents entry for the Crafting Arguments pages.

2. Cut out the title and glue it to the top of the page.

3. Cut out the *strong* label and glue it to the top-left side of the page. Cut out the *weak* label and glue it to the top-right side of the page.

4. Draw a line down the center of the page to create two columns. Discuss the kinds of arguments authors might employ and the kinds of techniques that create inherently stronger or weaker arguments.

5. Cut out the four flaps. Apply glue to the back of the top section of each flap. Attach the two strong argumentative techniques to the left side of the page. Attach the two weak argumentative techniques to the right side of the page.

6. Cut out the example statements. Glue each statement under the appropriate flap.

7. Write a statement at the bottom of the left column to explain what makes an argument strong. Write a statement at the bottom of the right column to explain what makes an argument weak.

Reflect on Learning

To complete the left-hand page, have students revisit their original argument. How many of the claims they made can be proven beyond a doubt? How many are not possible to prove? Have students list criteria they could look up to strengthen their arguments.

Crafting Arguments

using opinion	acknowledging opposition
accurate statistics	false comparison

Forty percent of dogs tested had the disease.	They make the best pizza in town.	They have the best-selling product of the year.	She will be a great leader because she is a good mother.
Although they are not foolproof, they do reduce injury in accidents.	This mop cleans floors better than the leading vacuum cleaner.	This is the worst movie ever made.	Even though their team is good, they sell less merchandise than several other teams.

Analyzing Argument

Have students anonymously describe something they strongly like or dislike on index cards. Collect the cards, shuffle them, and choose a few to read to the class. Have students explain whether each author likes or dislikes the item based on his word choice. Point out that authors do not have to explicitly state their feelings to make them clear; instead, they can use word choice and tone in addition to crafting a strong argument.

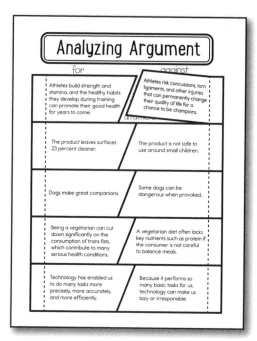

Creating the Notebook Page

Guide students through the following steps to complete the right-hand page in their notebooks.

1. Add a Table of Contents entry for the Analyzing Argument pages.

2. Cut out the title and glue it to the top of the page.

3. Draw a line down the center of the page to create two columns. Label the columns *for* and *against*.

4. Cut out the flaps. Pair the statements by topic. Read the statement on each flap and decide if it makes an argument for or against the topic. Apply glue to the back of left and right sections of each flap and attach the flaps to the page in the correct columns. The *for* and *against* arguments for the same topic should line up in the center.

5. Under each flap, write a sentence to explain how you know that the argument belongs in that column.

Reflect on Learning

To complete the left-hand page, have students write two statements. The first statement should provide an argument for the benefits of playing video games. The second statement should provide an argument against the effects of playing video games.

Analyzing Argument

Athletes build strength and stamina, and the healthy habits they develop during training can promote their good health for years to come.

Some dogs can be dangerous when provoked.

The product leaves surfaces 23 percent cleaner.

Because it performs so many basic tasks for us, technology can make us lazy or irresponsible.

Dogs make great companions.

The product is not safe to use around small children.

Being a vegetarian can cut down significantly on the consumption of trans fats, which contribute to many serious health conditions.

A vegetarian diet often lacks key nutrients such as protein if the consumer is not careful to balance meals.

Technology has enabled us to do many tasks more precisely, more accurately, and more efficiently.

Athletes risk concussions, torn ligaments, and other injuries that can permanently change their quality of life for a chance to be champions.

Conflicting Sources

Introduction

Have students role-play a situation in which two friends tell them conflicting stories about what they did the previous weekend. They should follow these story lines: one friend said on Friday that he was staying home all weekend; the other friend said they all met at the mall on Saturday. How will they figure out which story is true and what happened? Encourage students to evaluate the evidence in terms of the time line and to inspect the situation from multiple angles.

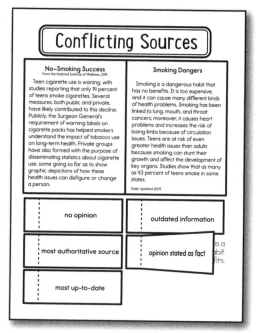

Creating the Notebook Page

Guide students through the following steps to complete the right-hand page in their notebooks.

1. Add a Table of Contents entry for the Conflicting Sources pages.

2. Cut out the title and glue it to the top of the page.

3. Cut out the two sources. Glue them side by side below the title.

4. Cut out the flaps. Read each source. Apply glue to the back of the left section of each flap and attach it below the source to which it applies.

5. Write the appropriate evidence from the source that supports each flap's placement.

Reflect on Learning

To complete the left-hand page, have students write a paragraph to explain a time when they heard two different sides of a story from two people. What ended up being the truth? How did they determine the truth?

Conflicting Sources

Smoking Dangers

Smoking is a dangerous habit that has no benefits. It is too expensive, and it can cause many different kinds of health problems. Smoking has been linked to lung, mouth, and throat cancers; moreover, it causes heart problems and increases the risk of losing limbs because of circulation issues. Teens are at risk of even greater health issues than adults because smoking can stunt their growth and affect the development of key organs. Studies show that as many as 43 percent of teens smoke in some states.

Date: Updated 2009

No-Smoking Success
From the National Institute of Wellness, 2014

Teen cigarette use is waning, with studies reporting that only 14 percent of teens smoke cigarettes. Several measures, both public and private, have likely contributed to this decline. Publicly, the Surgeon General's requirement of warning labels on cigarette packs has helped smokers understand the impact of tobacco use on long-term health. Private groups have also formed with the purpose of disseminating statistics about cigarette use, some going so far as to show graphic depictions of how these health issues can disfigure or change a person.

most authoritative source

no opinion

most up-to-date

outdated information

opinion stated as fact

Comparison and Connection

Introduction

Have students read two poems or other short passages that discuss the same topic from different perspectives. Ask students how the authors differ in their treatment of the subject, focusing on differences in word choice, tone, or theme as appropriate. Point out that even two authors writing about a subject with a similar purpose or theme in mind can still treat the subject differently; similarly, point out how two authors can use the same subject in ways that are so dramatically different that the pieces hardly seem related. This means that any attempt to compare and contrast items must look at both large and small details to get a complete picture of how the items are related.

Creating the Notebook Page

Guide students through the following steps to complete the right-hand page in their notebooks.

1. Add a Table of Contents entry for the Comparison and Connection pages.

2. Cut out the title and glue it to the top of the page.

3. Cut out the flaps. Apply glue to the back of the left section of the *Books* flap and attach it to the left side of the page. Apply glue to the back of the right section of the *Movies* flap and attach it to the right side of the page. Apply glue to the back of the top edge of the *Stories* flap and attach it so that it is centered in the cut-out space left between the other two flaps.

4. Cut out the detail pieces and glue each one under the appropriate flap. If a detail fits both books and movies, glue it under the *Stories* flap.

5. Below the *Books* and *Movies* flaps, write one more detail for each category.

Reflect on Learning

To complete the left-hand page, have students create a Venn diagram to compare and contrast two texts from the same genre.

Comparison and Connection

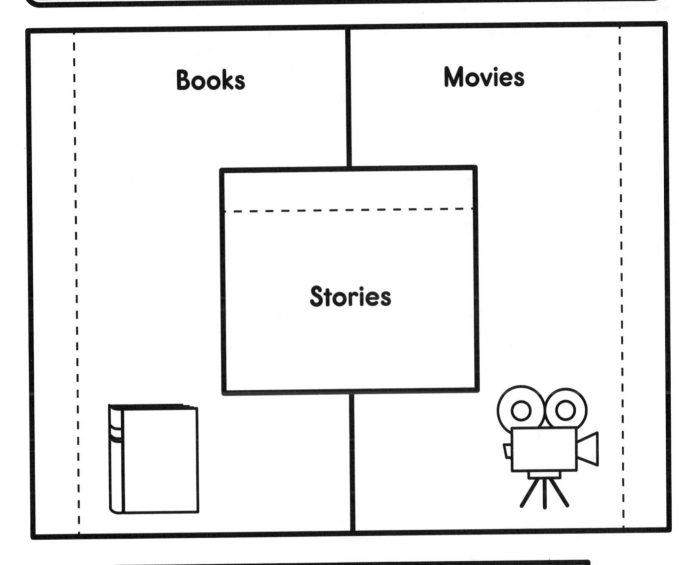

Books

Movies

Stories

have plot	can use music to help establish mood	can be used for entertainment or to inform	are easily annotated
easily convey characters' inner thoughts in words	rely primarily on dialogue	create uniform perceptions due to concrete representations	can be enjoyed without electricity

Prefixes and Suffixes

Introduction

Have students list multiple words that have the same letter groupings within them. Students should attempt to define the words and then decide what (if anything) the definitions have in common. Have students share their definitions with partners. Choose a few to display as examples to the class to show that knowing the definitions of prefixes, suffixes, and word roots can help them figure out new, unknown words.

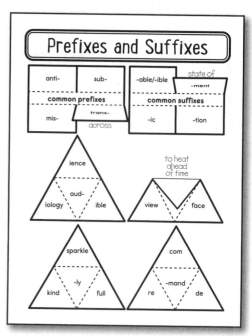

Creating the Notebook Page

Guide students through the following steps to complete the right-hand page in their notebooks.

1. Add a Table of Contents entry for the Prefixes and Suffixes pages.

2. Cut out the title and glue it to the top of the page.

3. Cut out the two rectangular flap books. Cut on the solid lines to create four flaps on each book. Apply glue to the back of the center sections and attach them side by side below the title.

4. Under each flap, write the definition of the word part.

5. Cut out the four triangular flap books. Apply glue to the back of the center sections and attach them to the page.

6. Under each flap, write the definition of the word that is formed by combining that flap with the prefix or suffix in the center of the triangular flap book.

Reflect on Learning

To complete the left-hand page, have students list as many words as possible that contain one of the prefixes or suffixes from the right-hand page. Have students choose several words to define, ensuring that the related definitions show the common influence of the prefix or suffix.

50

Prefixes and Suffixes

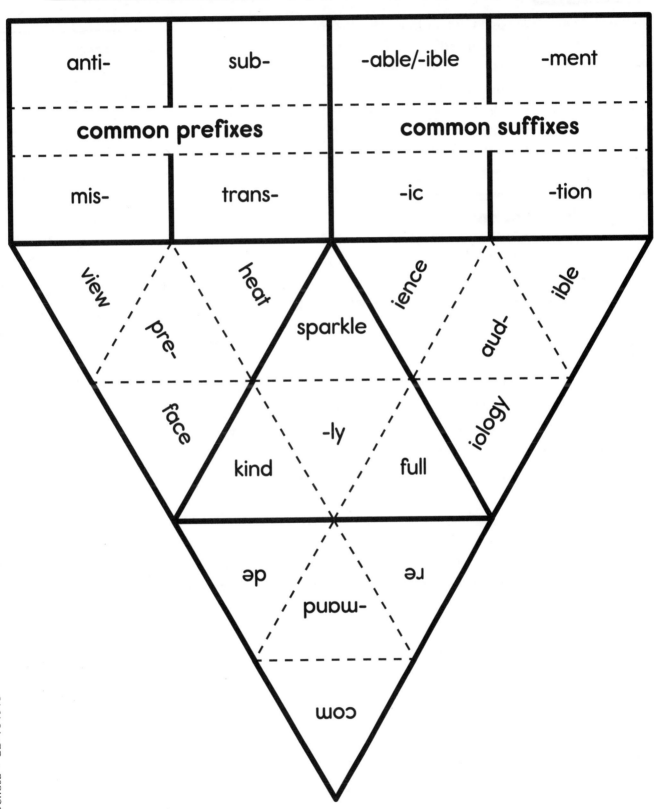

| anti- | sub- | -able/-ible | -ment |

common prefixes | **common suffixes**

| mis- | trans- | -ic | -tion |

view | heat | ience | ible

pre-

sparkle

aud-

face

-ly

iology

kind | full

de | re

-mand

com

Word Parts

Introduction

Divide the class into groups of three or four. Ask students to brainstorm as many prefixes and suffixes as they can in three minutes. Generate a list of some of the groups' prefixes and suffixes on the board. Discuss the definitions of the affixes. Then, have the groups use root words to construct words with a prefix and a suffix. The students should write their new words and the meaning of each one on chart paper. Display the charts around the room as a reference.

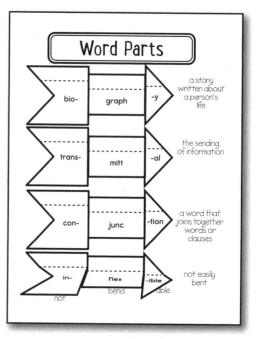

Creating the Notebook Page

Guide students through the following steps to complete the right-hand page in their notebooks.

1. Add a Table of Contents entry for the Word Parts pages.

2. Cut out the title and glue it to the top of the page.

3. Cut out the 12 flaps. Form arrows using three flaps for each arrow (one of each shape). Arrange the flaps so that each arrow creates a word. Apply glue to the back of the top section of each flap and attach the flaps to the page.

4. Under each flap, write the definition of the word part. At the tip of each arrow, write the definition of the new word formed by putting the pieces together.

Reflect on Learning

To complete the left-hand page, have students divide their page into three columns labeled *prefix*, *root*, *suffix*. Students should look through classroom materials to find unfamiliar words that have these three word parts. Students should write each part of the word in the correct column. Then have students use the word parts to define each word.

Word Parts

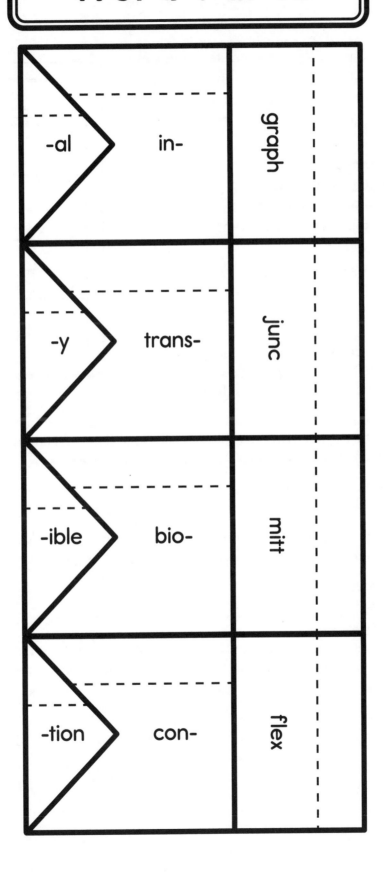

-al	in-	graph
-y	trans-	junc
-ible	bio-	mitt
-tion	con-	flex

Word Choice

Introduction

Show students an image and have them write several sentences to describe it. Have students share their descriptions, asking other students whether each description is positive, negative, or neutral. Ask them what words in the descriptions helped them recognize the tone.

Creating the Notebook Page

Guide students through the following steps to complete the right-hand page in their notebooks.

1. Add a Table of Contents entry for the Word Choice pages.

2. Cut out the title and glue it to the top of the page.

3. Cut out the *How can rephrasing* flap book. Cut on the solid line to create two flaps. Apply glue to the back of the top section and attach it below the title.

4. Under the *emphasis* flap, explain how a sentence can be rephrased to move emphasis toward or away from particular words. Under the *mood or tone* flap, explain how rephrasing a sentence can change the way the message is intended or understood.

5. Cut out the large flap book. Cut on the solid lines to create six flaps. Apply glue to the back of the center section and attach it to the page.

6. Read the sentences on the left flaps. Under each flap, explain how the variations in word choice or sentence structure change what is emphasized or implied. Repeat with the right flaps.

Reflect on Learning

To complete the left-hand page, have students write two short paragraphs. One should focus on what went right for the student throughout the day, and the other should focus on what may have happened to them or what other people did throughout the day. Students should use words in their paragraphs that express mood and tone.

Word Choice

How can rephrasing a sentence change

emphasis?	mood or tone?

The vase was broken.	**What is the**	We talked for hours.
The vase was destroyed.	**e f f e c t**	We gossiped for hours.
The vase broke.	**of each change**	The discussion went on for hours.

Similar Words

Introduction

Have students draw a monster. Be intentionally vague to allow for creativity. At the top of a second sheet of paper, have students describe their monsters. Have students work with partners and trade descriptions. Partners should then try to re-create each other's monsters based on the descriptions and then compare their drawings to the originals. Have students discuss what caused any differences between the two drawings. Point out how language precision affects communication.

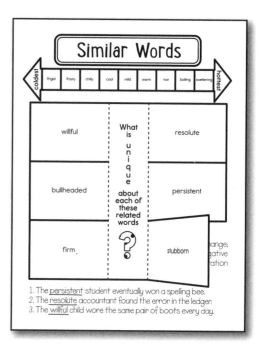

Creating the Notebook Page

Guide students through the following steps to complete the right-hand page in their notebooks.

1. Add a Table of Contents entry for the Similar Words pages.

2. Cut out the title and glue it to the top of the page.

3. Cut out the arrow and glue it horizontally below the title.

4. Cut out the words and glue them on the arrow in order from coldest to hottest. Discuss how synonyms can have shades of meaning.

4. Cut out the flap book. Cut on the solid lines to create six flaps. Apply glue to the back of the center section and attach it below the arrow.

5. Under each flap, describe how that word is different from the words on the other flaps.

6. Choose three words from the flap book to use in sentences at the bottom of the page. Make sure the sentences reflect the slight differences in the meaning of the words.

Reflect on Learning

To complete the left-hand page, have students write a paragraph to describe a person, place, or thing as precisely as possible. Have students underline or highlight the specific words that give precise details.

Similar Words

| hot | cool | frosty | boiling | mild | chilly | sweltering | warm | frigid |

willful	What is **u n i q u e** about each of these related words 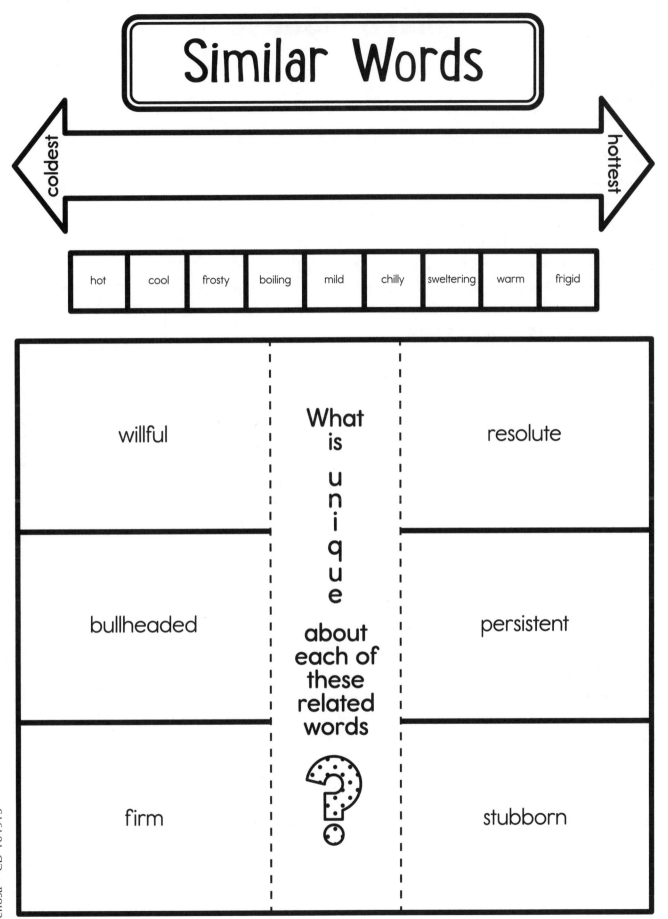	resolute
bullheaded		persistent
firm		stubborn

Verb Moods

Introduction

Use imperative verbs to have students perform tasks (for example, "stand up," "raise your hand," "sit down," "clap three times") individually and as a group. Ask students to explain how they know that the sentences in question are commands and not questions. Define the four verb moods on the board: interrogative (asking a question), indicative (stating a fact or idea or giving detail), imperative (giving a command), and subjunctive (depending on something else—if this, then that).

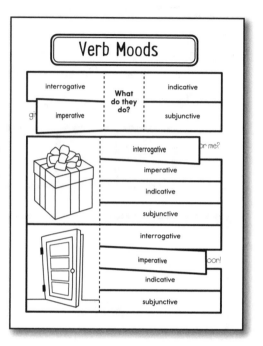

Creating the Notebook Page

Guide students through the following steps to complete the right-hand page in their notebooks.

1. Add a Table of Contents entry for the Verb Moods pages.

2. Cut out the title and glue it to the top of the page.

3. Cut out the *What do they do?* flap book. Cut on the solid lines to create four flaps. Apply glue to the back of the center section and attach it below the title.

4. Under each verb mood, write the definition.

5. Cut out the two picture flap books. Cut on the solid lines to create four flaps on each book. Apply glue to the back of the left sections and attach them to the bottom of the page.

6. Under each flap, write a sentence about the picture in the indicated mood.

Reflect on Learning

To complete the left-hand page, have students write a paragraph about their school day. The paragraph should include the four types of verbs. Sutdents should label the verbs used.

Verb Moods

interrogative		indicative
	What do they do?	
imperative		subjunctive

	interrogative
	imperative
	indicative
	subjunctive

	interrogative
	imperative
	indicative
	subjunctive

Active and Passive Voice

Introduction

Have students explain the difference between two sentences written on the board: *My sister broke the vase* and *The vase was broken by my sister.* Make sure students recognize the difference in emphasis (the perpetrator vs. the incident). Have students write a note to their parents to explain how something happened in a way that deflects blame with passive structure (for example, *Where did all the cookies go?* or *What is all over the carpet?*). Then, have students write a second explanation note to their parents that assigns blame with active structure.

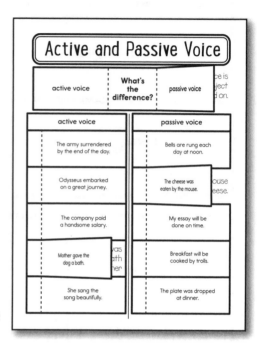

Creating the Notebook Page

Guide students through the following steps to complete the right-hand page in their notebooks.

1. Add a Table of Contents entry for the Active and Passive Voice pages.

2. Cut out the title and glue it to the top of the page.

3. Cut out the *What's the Difference?* flap book. Apply glue to the back of the center section and attach it below the title.

4. Explain how to identify active voice under the *active voice* flap. Explain how to identify passive voice under the *passive voice* flap.

5. Draw a line down the center of the page to divide it into two columns.

6. Cut out the *active voice* and *passive voice* labels. Glue one at the top of each column.

7. Cut out the flaps. Apply glue to the back of each left section and attach each sentence in the column that represents the current voice (active or passive).

8. Under each flap, rewrite the sentence in the opposite voice.

Reflect on Learning

To complete the left-hand page, have students write a paragraph about their favorite social studies topic. Then, have students rewrite the paragraph with each verb switched to the opposite tense (verbs that were active in the first paragraph should be passive in the second and vice versa). Have students write a sentence explaining the difference between the paragraphs (is one clearer than the other? is one more concise?).

Active and Passive Voice

active voice	What's the difference?	passive voice

active voice	passive voice
The cheese was eaten by the mouse.	She sang the song beautifully.
Mother gave the dog a bath.	The plate was dropped at dinner.
The company paid a handsome salary.	Breakfast will be cooked by trolls.
Odysseus embarked on a great journey.	My essay will be done on time.
Bells are rung each day at noon.	The army surrendered by the end of the day.

Verbals

Introduction

Review or define verbals: verbs that are used as different parts of speech such as gerunds, participles, and infinitives. Have students illustrate a gerund (running, talking, showing, writing). Write sentences on the board using the words students illustrated as gerunds. Instead of writing the words, tape students' drawings in place of the words on the board. Show how the words students might typically identify as "verbs" could be replaced by nouns in these situations, meaning that they are acting as nouns. Do the same exercise to show that participles can be replaced by adjectives. Show students how to form infinitives and show that those can be plugged into different points in a sentence as well, acting as several different parts of speech.

Creating the Notebook Page

Guide students through the following steps to complete the right-hand page in their notebooks.

1. Add a Table of Contents entry for the Verbals pages.

2. Cut out the title and glue it to the top of the page.

3. Cut out the flap book. Cut on the solid lines to create six flaps. Apply glue to the back of the left and center sections and attach the flap book below the title.

4. For the top row of flaps, write the typical form (adding -ing or -ed or starts with to) of each kind of verbal under the flap. For the bottom row of flaps, explain what part of speech each verbal becomes.

5. Cut out the three examples of flaps. Apply glue to the back of the top section of each flap and attach the flaps below the flap book.

6. Cut out the example phrases and glue them under the appropriate flap.

7. Underline the verbals in each example phrase.

Reflect on Learning

To complete the left-hand page, have students take one verb and write sentences using it as a verb, gerund, infinitive, and participle.

Verbals

form	add	add	starts with
	⌐ gerunds ⌐	⌐ participles ⌐	⌐ infinitives ⌐
used as	a	an	a

examples of	examples of	examples of
gerunds	**participles**	**infinitives**

Swimming is a hobby.	a long way to run	time to go	a ripped cloth	I like her singing.	the highlighted text	the running car	The candidate is in the running.	wanting to fly

Commas

Introduction

Have students write a short essay about any topic. Then, have them create footnotes to explain why they used each comma they included. If they cannot explain why they used a particular comma, have them ask a neighbor whether that comma was appropriate. Help point students in the right direction as they complete this portion, as they likely will not be able to correctly analyze every comma they used. Use their words to write a few basic comma rules on the board.

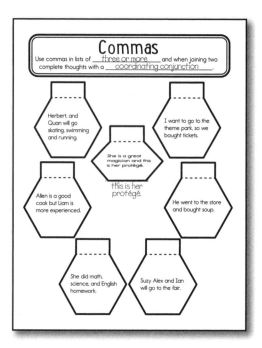

Creating the Notebook Page

Guide students through the following steps to complete the right-hand page in their notebooks.

1. Add a Table of Contents entry for the Commas pages.

2. Cut out the title and glue it to the top of the page.

3. Complete the explanation. (Use commas in lists of **three or more** and when joining two complete thoughts with a **coordinating conjunction**.) Remind students of the FANBOYS mnemonic for coordinating conjunctions: *for, and, nor, but, or, yet,* and *so.*

4. Cut out the flaps. Apply glue to the back of the top sections and attach them to the page.

5. Under each flap, write whether the use of commas in the sentence is correct. If it is correct, explain why; if it is not, write the sentence correctly.

Reflect on Learning

To complete the left-hand page, have students revisit their original paragraphs. Were any commas wrong in the original? If so, what should have been done? Were there any places that should have had commas that did not? Were there any correct commas that were not adequately explained before that can be explained now? Next, have students take two simple thoughts from their original paragraphs and write them as one sentence using appropriate punctuation.

Commas

Use commas in lists of _____ and when joining two complete thoughts with a _____.

Suzy Alex and Ian will go to the fair.

She did math, science, and English homework.

I want to go to the theme park, so we bought tickets.

He went to the store and bought soup.

She is a great magician and this is her protégé.

Allen is a good cook but Liam is more experienced.

Herbert, and Quan will go skating, swimming and running.

Revising and Editing

Introduction

Give students an article with several different types of errors (grammatical, organizational, and clarity). Ask students to pinpoint things they think are wrong or awkward. As they find issues, model how to correct them on the board. Have students rewrite the corrected version you create as a class under the original, underlining fixed sentences and annotating why the changes made were appropriate.

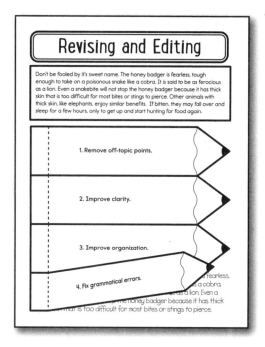

Creating the Notebook Page

Guide students through the following steps to complete the right-hand page in their notebooks.

1. Add a Table of Contents entry for the Revising and Editing pages.

2. Cut out the title and glue it to the top of the page.

3. Cut out the passage and glue it below the title.

4. Cut out the four flaps. Apply glue to the back of the left sections and attach them to the page in order. The flaps should not overlap.

5. Under the *Remove off-topic points* flap, write a new version of the original passage that deletes irrelevant details.

6. Under the *Improve clarity* flap, write a new version of the passage from the previous step that clarifies any vague or disjointed points.

7. Under the *Improve organization* flap, write a new version of the passage from the previous step that is more organized.

8. Under the *Fix grammatical errors* flap, finalize the new version you have created by ensuring it is free of grammatical errors.

Reflect on Learning

To complete the left-hand page, have students write a how-to column with partners to explain how to "Edit an Essay Like [partner's name]." Students should interview their partners about the editing techniques they use, don't use, or think they should use. The column should stylistically resemble either a gossip column or an advice column. Then, have students exchange notebooks with their partners and offer revision advice based on the steps on the right-hand page.

Revising and Editing

Don't be fooled by it's sweet name. The honey badger is fearless, tough enough to take on a poisonous snake like a cobra. It is said to be as ferocious as a lion. Even a snakebite will not stop the honey badger because it has thick skin that is too difficult for most bites or stings to pierce. Other animals with thick skin, like elephants, enjoy similar benefits. If bitten, they may fall over and sleep for a few hours, only to get up and start hunting for food again.

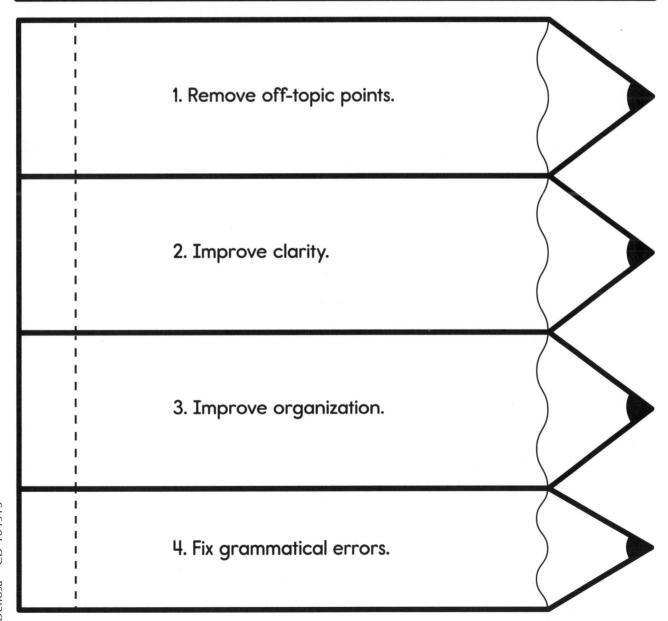

1. Remove off-topic points.

2. Improve clarity.

3. Improve organization.

4. Fix grammatical errors.

Organization and Transitions

Introduction

Give students several sentence strips that work in a few different orders. Have students organize the sentences, adding transition words between the sentences where necessary. Then, have students compare their paragraphs. Discuss with students the author's ability to manipulate sentences and transitions to make different organization options as well as give examples of different organizational structures (chronological, limiting to one point of view, pro/con, etc.). Give examples of transition words such as *next* or *therefore* and show how they clearly indicate what the author is doing.

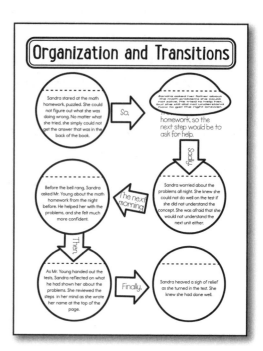

Creating the Notebook Page

Guide students through the following steps to complete the right-hand page in their notebooks.

1. Add a Table of Contents entry for the Organization and Transitions pages.

2. Cut out the title and glue it to the top of the page.

3. Cut out the sentence flaps and arrows. Read the sentences. Apply glue to the back of the top sections of the sentence flaps and attach them in a natural order like a flowchart. Apply glue to the back of the arrows and attach them to the page to show the progression of thoughts.

4. Under each flap, write why that sentence belongs in that position as opposed to any other.

5. On the arrows, write transition words or phrases that will improve the clarity of the organization.

Reflect on Learning

To complete the left-hand page, have students create a time line that shows the progression of a specific day or event. Have students rewrite the information from the time line as a paragraph that uses specific transition words and phrases to connect the events from the time line.

Organization and Transitions

Before the bell rang, Sandra asked Mr. Young about the math homework from the night before. He helped her with the problems, and she felt much more confident.

Sandra heaved a sigh of relief as she turned in the test. She knew she had done well.

Sandra stared at the math homework, puzzled. She could not figure out what she was doing wrong. No matter what she tried, she simply could not get the answer that was in the back of the book.

As Mr. Young handed out the tests, Sandra reflected on what he had shown her about the problems. She reviewed the steps in her mind as she wrote her name at the top of the page.

Sandra asked her father about the math problems she could not solve. He tried to help her, but she still did not understand how to get the right answer.

Sandra worried about the problems all night. She knew she could not do well on the test if she did not understand the concept. She was afraid that she would not understand the next unit either.

Organizing Details

Introduction

Create a flowchart on the board that shows an introduction, three body paragraphs, and a conclusion. Give students a topic, such as "leadership," and have them write details on self-stick notes. Have students place them in the appropriate sections of the flowchart. As they read through their "essays," allow them to relocate, add, or remove details as desired. Discuss the kinds of details that work well for each kind of paragraph in most essays.

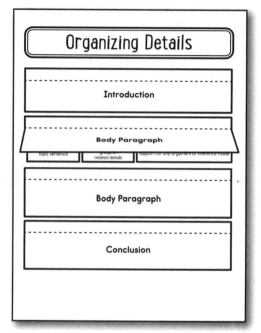

Creating the Notebook Page

Guide students through the following steps to complete the right-hand page in their notebooks.

1. Add a Table of Contents entry for the Organizing Details pages.

2. Cut out the title and glue it to the top of the page.

3. Cut out the four flaps. Apply glue to the back of the top sections and attach them to the page in the order the paragraphs should appear.

4. Cut out the details and glue them under the appropriate flaps. If a detail could fit in more than one paragraph, consider where it would most often be the most effective.

Reflect on Learning

To complete the left-hand page, have students outline an essay that defines freedom using the examples from the right-hand page as a starting point.

Organizing Details

Introduction

Body Paragraph

Conclusion

Body Paragraph

definition of word or topic	topic sentence	topic sentence	summary of previous information
general background information	group of related details	group of related details	overview that completely avoids introducing new information
support for any argument or inference made		support for any argument or inference made	

Fictional Perspectives

Introduction

Have students read a short story and then write a paragraph to explain how the story would be different if told from a different point of view, if a narrator were added or taken away, or if the order of events was changed. Discuss with students how authors can make these choices intentionally to create more engaging, relatable, or understandable stories.

Creating the Notebook Page

Guide students through the following steps to complete the right-hand page in their notebooks.

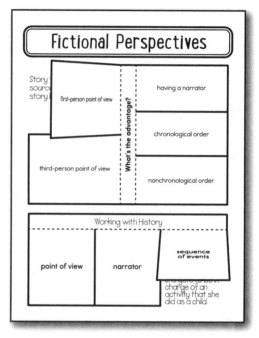

1. Add a Table of Contents entry for the Fictional Perspectives pages.

2. Cut out the title and glue it to the top of the page.

3. Cut out the large flap book and cut on the solid lines to create five flaps. Apply glue to the back of the middle section and attach it below the title.

4. Under each flap, write the advantage an author can gain by using that particular tactic.

5. Cut out the smaller flap book and cut on the solid lines to create three flaps. Apply glue to the back of the top section and attach it to the bottom of the page.

6. Write the name of a story recently read in class on the top of the flap book. Use details from the story to describe why the author chose the point of view, narrator (or lack thereof), and story order used in the work.

Reflect on Learning

To complete the left-hand page, have students plan a short story. The plan should include a general premise (a character or a few main characters and a conflict), what point of view the story will use and why, whether the story will have a narrator and why, and whether the story will be told in chronological order and why.

Fictional Perspectives

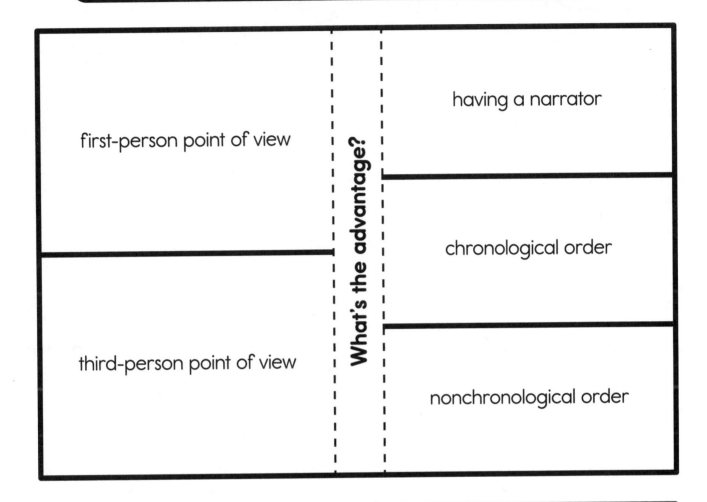

first-person point of view

third-person point of view

What's the advantage?

having a narrator

chronological order

nonchronological order

point of view

narrator

sequence of events

Flawed Logic

Introduction

Have students attempt to convince their closest classmates of something that absolutely can't be proven because it is an opinion. Possible topics include the best sports team ever, the worst cafeteria food, or the most exciting movie ever made. Have students record some of the persuasive tactics their classmates use and whether those appeals were effective. They should also note whether they agreed with the opinions before their classmates began their speeches. Have students discuss the following questions: Why did they tend to find the arguments of people with whom they already agreed more effective? Why is the opposite also true? What does this reveal about these kinds of arguments?

Creating the Notebook Page

Guide students through the following steps to complete the right-hand page in their notebooks.

1. Add a Table of Contents entry for the Flawed Logic pages.

2. Cut out the title and glue it to the top of the page.

3. Cut out the flaps. Apply glue to the back of the left sections and attach them to the page.

4. Under each flap, explain why the original conclusion is flawed and write a new conclusion that is more accurate for the same evidence.

Reflect on Learning

To complete the left-hand page, have students write an "argue-proof argument" that only uses concrete, logical support.

Flawed Logic

Evidence: It is not the most popular brand by sales.

Conclusion: It is not an effective product.

Evidence: He is ahead of other candidates in a poll.

Conclusion: Many people like him.

Evidence: The team lost the game.

Conclusion: They are not good players.

Evidence: My brother got sick after doing what you are doing.

Conclusion: You will get sick too.

Evidence: She did not come to our party.

Conclusion: She does not like us.

Writing with Purpose

Review theme, characterization, setting, and conflict. Point out to students that most details in a text serve to establish or further one of these four elements. Define "author's purpose" as an author's intended effect of a detail on the story or message behind a story. Then, have students read a short story and label each paragraph with colored tabs or self-stick notes to indicate whether it is very important, somewhat important, or not important. Have students choose a few answers to explain (why was that paragraph very important? why wasn't another as vital?). Discuss the effect that removing the paragraph in question might have on the text to further drive the point. Would excluding that detail affect an important characterization, change the setting or conflict, or modify the theme?

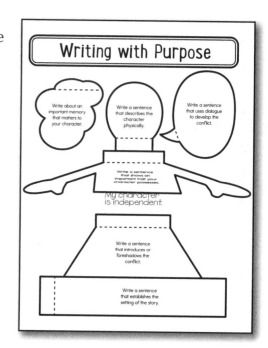

Creating the Notebook Page

Guide students through the following steps to complete the right-hand page in their notebooks.

1. Add a Table of Contents entry for the Writing with Purpose pages.

2. Cut out the title and glue it to the top of the page.

3. Cut out the flaps. Apply glue to the back of the tabs and attach them to the page so that they create an image of a person standing on a base with a speech bubble and a thought bubble.

4. Imagine a story loosely based on your life and follow the instructions on the flaps to introduce yourself as the character in that story.

Reflect on Learning

To complete the left-hand page, consider the writer's purpose and write a story that includes the sentences from the right-hand page.

Writing with Purpose

Write about an important memory that matters to your character.

Write a sentence that describes the character physically.

Write a sentence that uses dialogue to develop the conflict.

Write a sentence that shows an important trait your character possesses.

Write a sentence that introduces or foreshadows the conflict.

Write a sentence that establishes the setting of the story.

Tabs

Cut out each tab and label it. Apply glue to the back of each tab and align it on the outside edge of the page with only the label section showing beyond the edge. Then, fold each tab to seal the page inside.

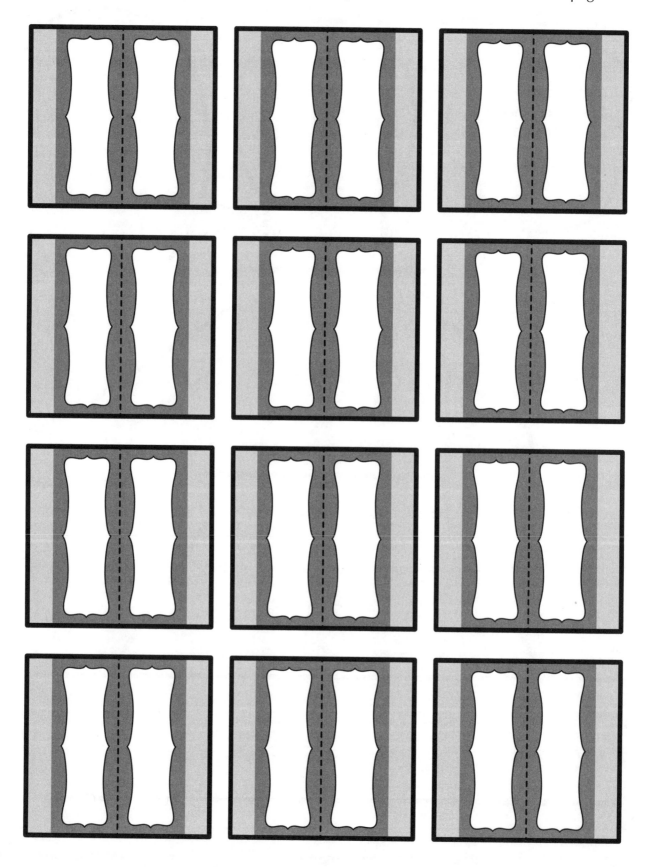

Cut out the KWL chart and cut on the solid lines to create three separate flaps. Apply glue to the back of the Topic section to attach the chart to a notebook page.

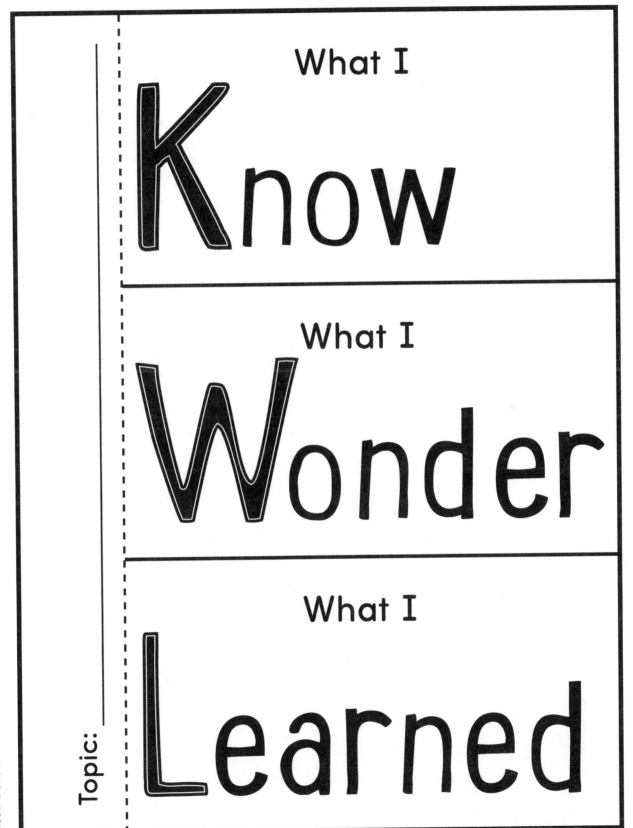

Topic:

What I

Know

What I

Wonder

What I

Learned

Library Pocket

Cut out the library pocket on the solid lines. Fold in the side tabs and apply glue to them before folding up the front of the pocket. Apply glue to the back of the pocket to attach it to a notebook page.

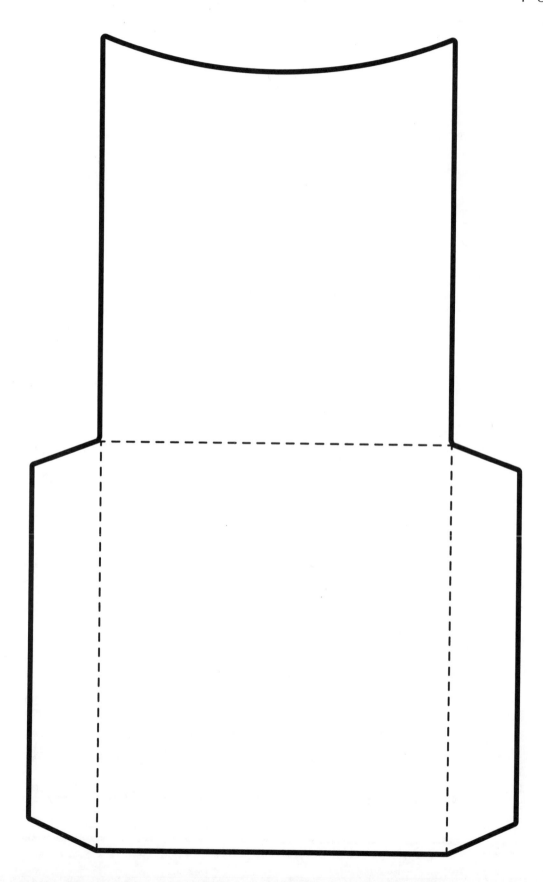

Envelope

Cut out the envelope on the solid lines. Fold in the side tabs and apply glue to them before folding up the rectangular front of the envelope. Fold down the triangular flap to close the envelope. Apply glue to the back of the envelope to attach it to a notebook page.

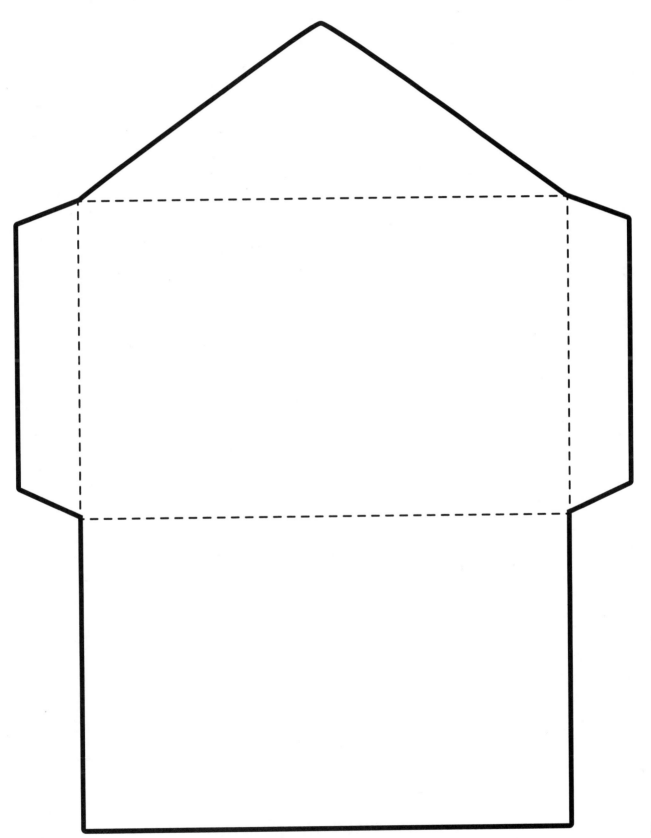

Pocket and Cards

Cut out the pocket on the solid lines. Fold over the front of the pocket. Then, apply glue to the tabs and fold them around the back of the pocket. Apply glue to the back of the pocket to attach it to a notebook page. Cut out the cards and store them in the envelope.

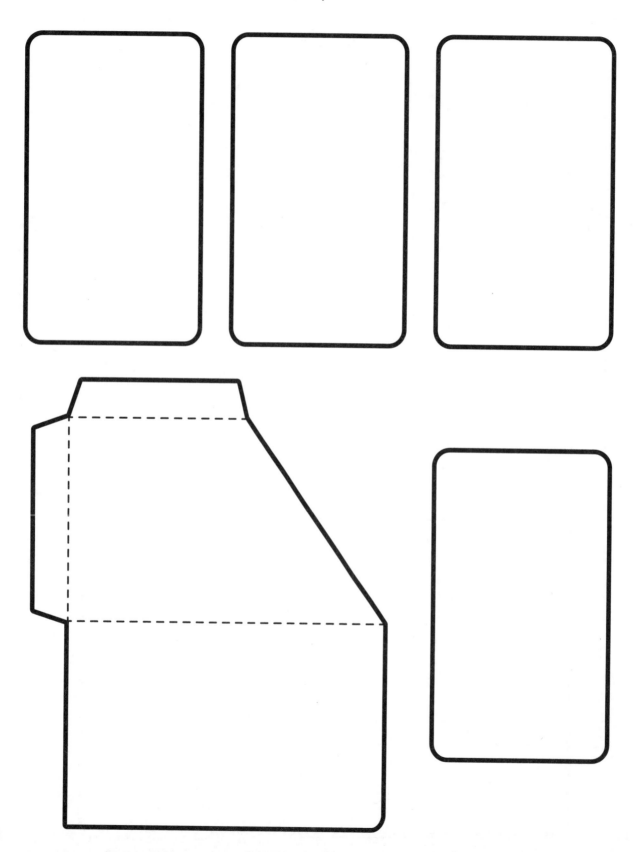

Six-Flap Shutter Fold

Cut out the shutter fold around the outside border. Then, cut on the solid lines to create six flaps. Fold the flaps toward the center. Apply glue to the back of the shutter fold to attach it to a notebook page.

If desired, this template can be modified to create a four-flap shutter fold by cutting off the bottom row. You can also create two three-flap books by cutting it in half down the center line.

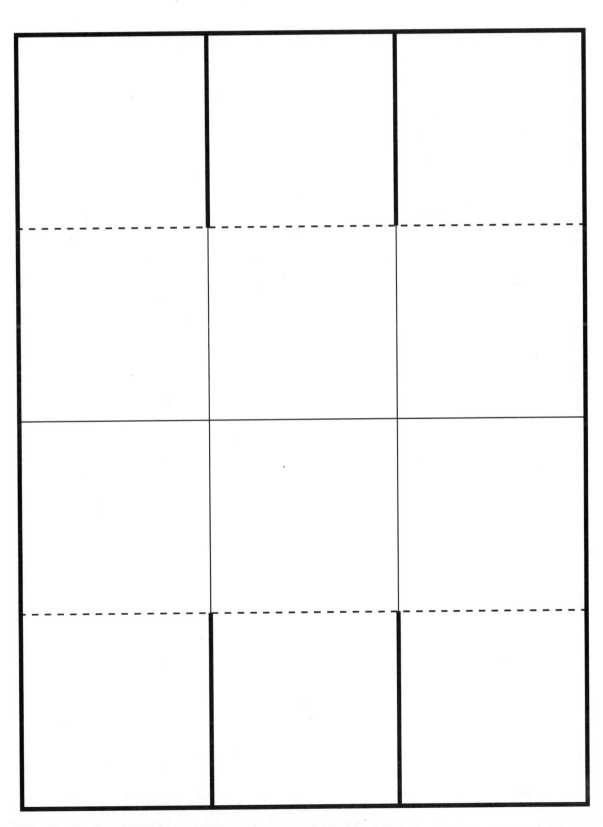

Eight-Flap Shutter Fold

Cut out the shutter fold around the outside border. Then, cut on the solid lines to create eight flaps. Fold the flaps toward the center. Apply glue to the back of the shutter fold to attach it to a notebook page.

If desired, this template can be modified to create two four-flap shutter folds by cutting off the bottom two rows. You can also create two four-flap books by cutting it in half down the center line.

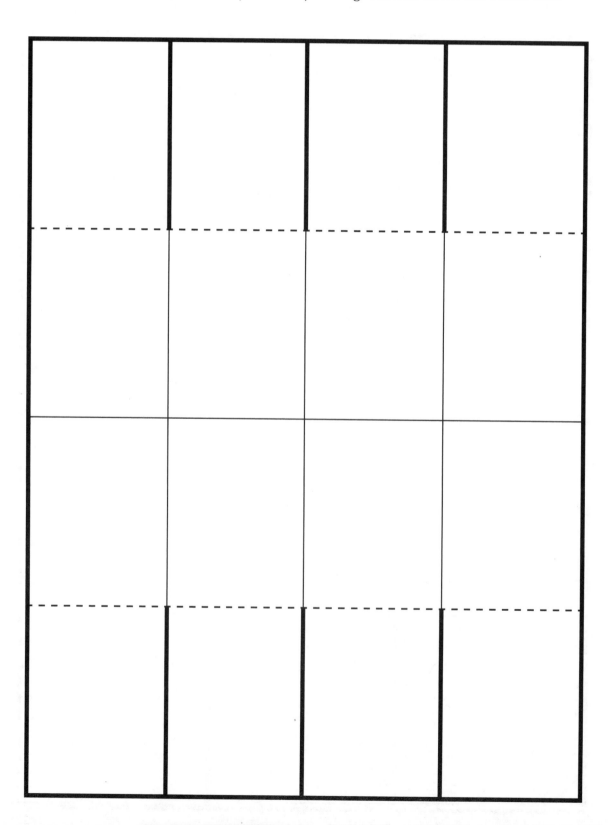

Flap Book—Eight Flaps

Cut out the flap book around the outside border. Then, cut on the solid lines to create eight flaps. Apply glue to the back of the center section to attach it to a notebook page.

If desired, this template can be modified to create a six-flap or two four-flap books by cutting off the bottom row or two. You can also create a tall four-flap book by cutting off the flaps on the left side.

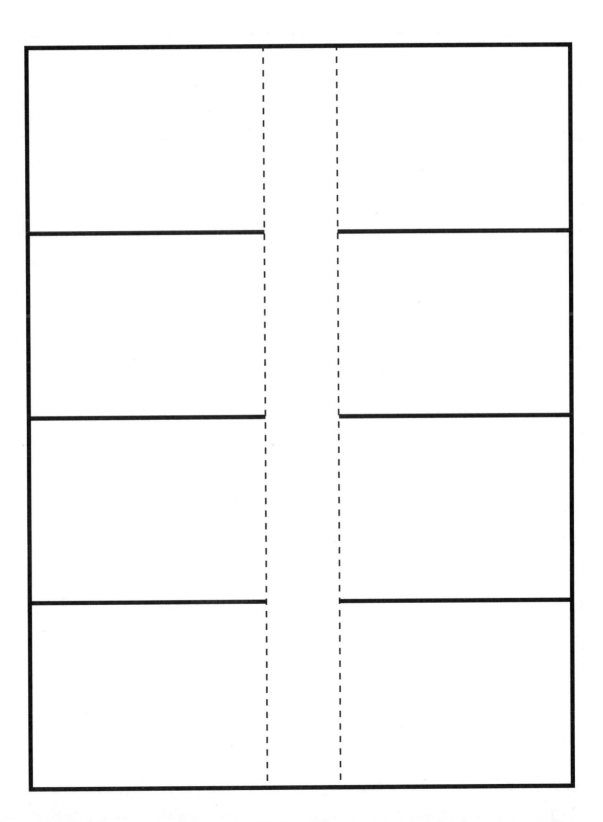

Flap Book—Twelve Flaps

Cut out the flap book around the outside border. Then, cut on the solid lines to create 12 flaps. Apply glue to the back of the center section to attach it to a notebook page.

If desired, this template can be modified to create smaller flap books by cutting off any number of rows from the bottom. You can also create a tall flap book by cutting off the flaps on the left side.

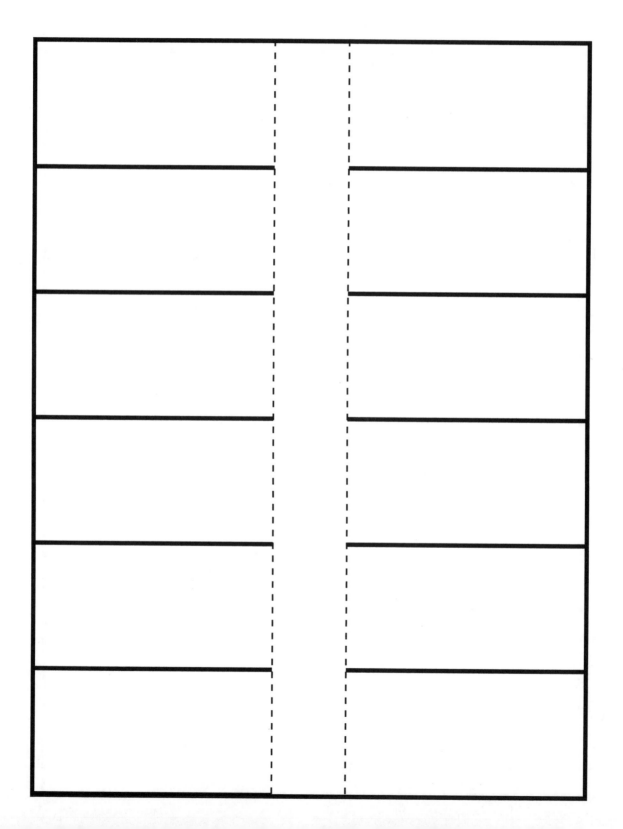

Shaped Flaps

Cut out each shaped flap. Apply glue to the back of the narrow section to attach it to a notebook page.

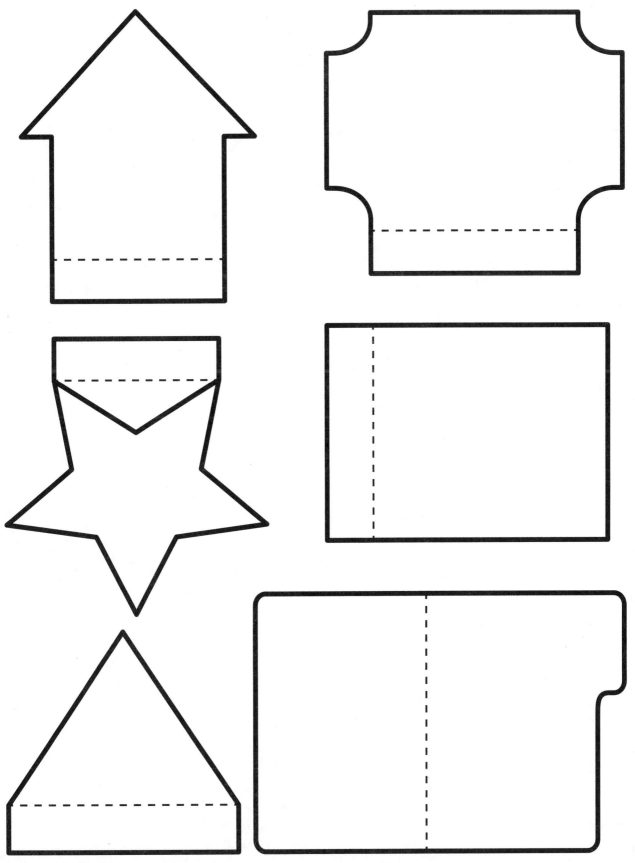

Shaped Flaps

Interlocking Booklet

Cut out the booklet on the solid lines, including the short vertical lines on the top and bottom flaps. Then, fold the top and bottom flaps toward the center, interlocking them using the small vertical cuts. Apply glue to the back of the center panel to attach it to a notebook page.

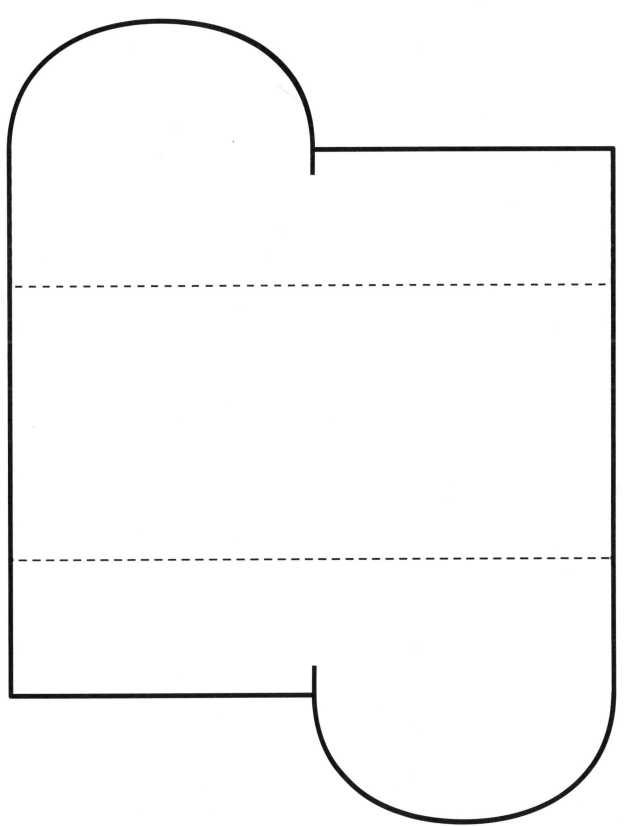

Four-Flap Petal Fold

Cut out the shape on the solid lines. Then, fold the flaps toward the center. Apply glue to the back of the center panel to attach it to a notebook page.

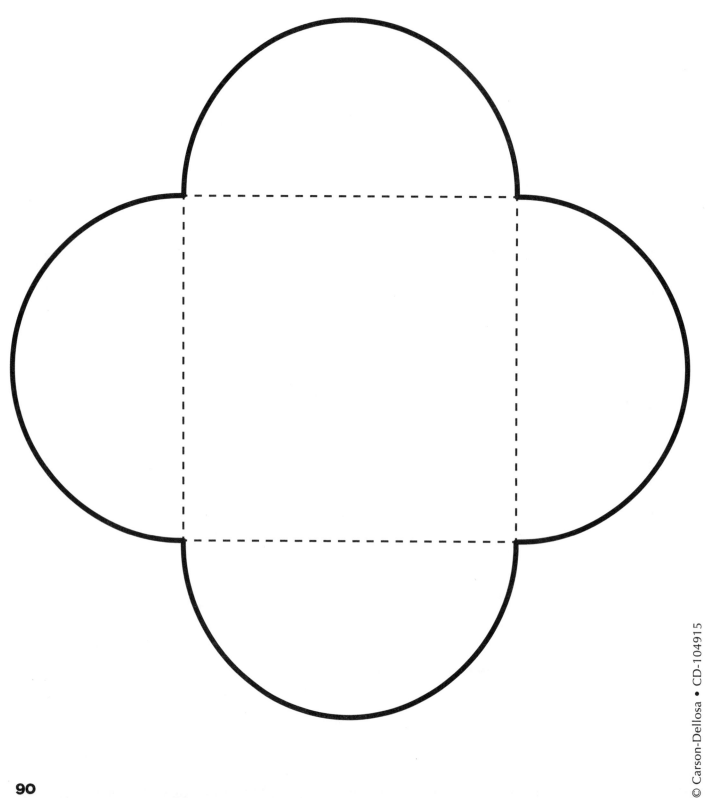

Six-Flap Petal Fold

Cut out the shape on the solid lines. Then, fold the flaps toward the center and back out. Apply glue to the back of the center panel to attach it to a notebook page.

Accordion Folds

Cut out the accordion pieces on the solid lines. Fold on the dashed lines, alternating the fold direction. Apply glue to the back of the last section to attach it to a notebook page.

You may modify the accordion books to have more or fewer pages by cutting off extra pages or by having students glue the first and last panels of two accordion books together.

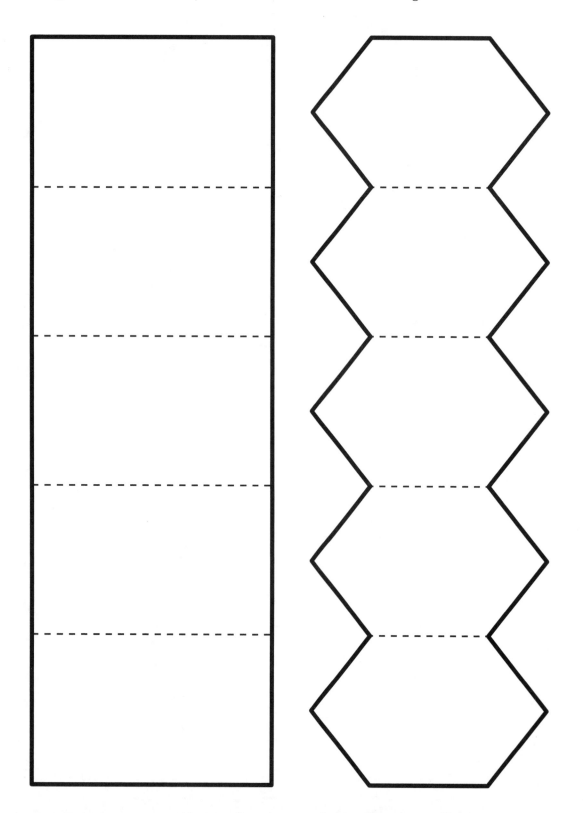

Accordion Folds

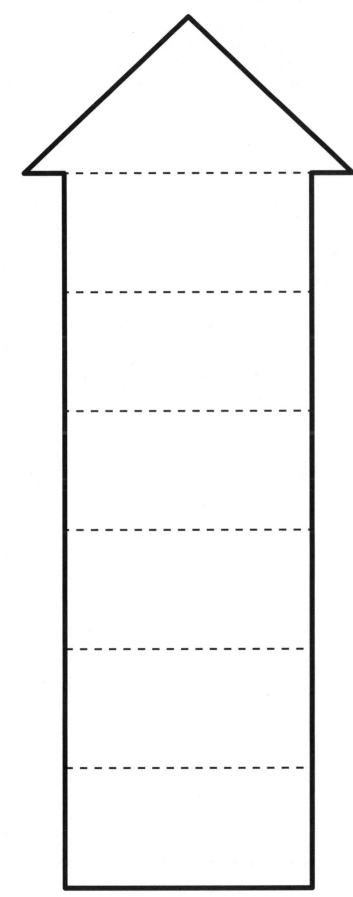

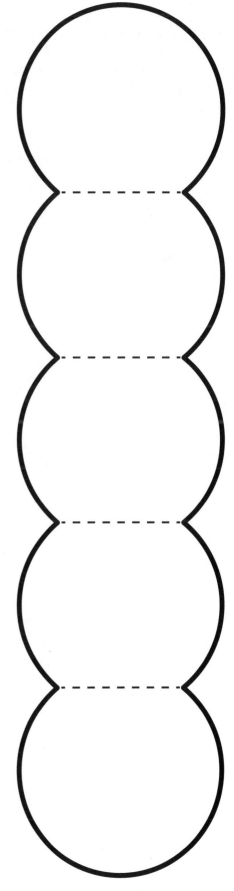

Clamshell Fold

Cut out the clamshell fold on the solid lines. Fold and unfold the piece on the three dashed lines. With the piece oriented so that the folds form an X with a horizontal line through it, pull the left and right sides together at the fold line. Then, keeping the sides touching, bring the top edge down to meet the bottom edge. You should be left with a triangular shape that unfolds into a square. Apply glue to the back of the triangle to attach the clamshell to a notebook page.

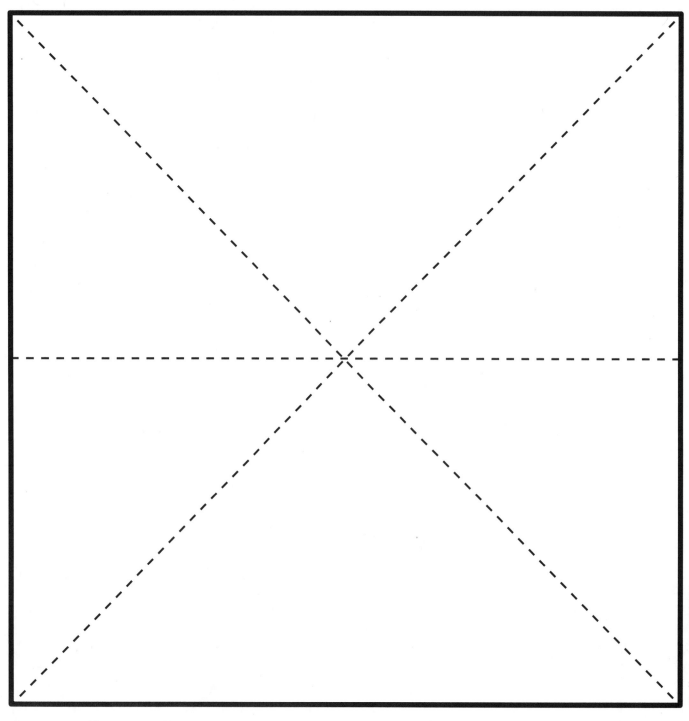

Puzzle Pieces

Cut out each puzzle along the solid lines to create a three- or four-piece puzzle. Apply glue to the back of each puzzle piece to attach it to a notebook page. Alternately, apply glue only to one edge of each piece to create flaps.

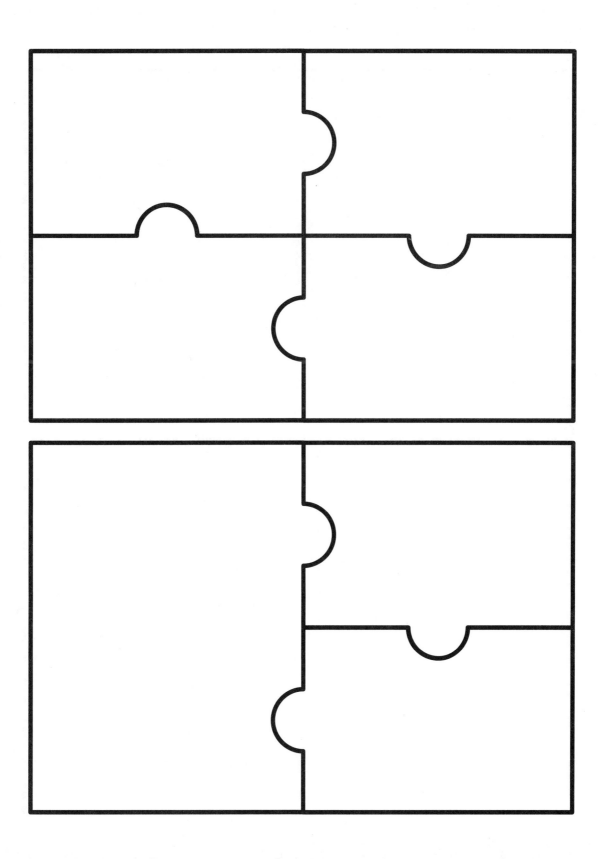

Flip Book

Cut out the two rectangular pieces on the solid lines. Fold each rectangle on the dashed lines. Fold the piece with the gray glue section so that it is inside the fold. Apply glue to the gray glue section and place the other folded rectangle on top so that the folds are nested and create a book with four cascading flaps. Make sure that the inside pages are facing up so that the edges of both pages are visible. Apply glue to the back of the book to attach it to a notebook page.

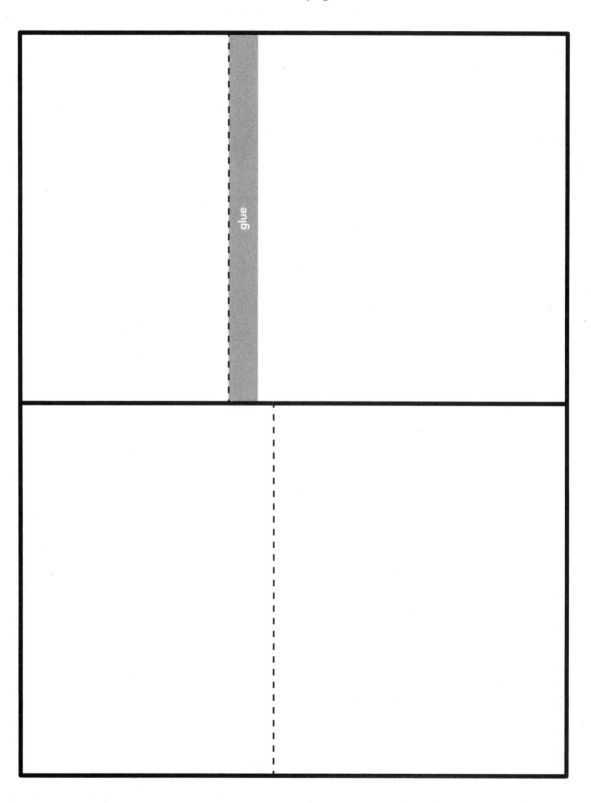